MW01245401

TRUSTING THROUGH
THE DARKNESS

TRUSTING THROUGH THE DARKNESS

Biblical Wisdom and Inspiration

Dr. Andrew Robinson
Wanda Kay Robinson

Copyright © 2023

Nearly all Scriptures taken from the Augmented King James
Version Bible and a few from the King James Version Bible.
Published by Christ Ministries Inc.
Charleston, Illinois 61920
ChristMinistriesInc.org
ActsChristMinistries@gmail.com
ISBN: 9798849513379

Table of Contents

Dedication

This Book is dedicated to our Christ Ministries Inc. family of ministers, most of whom we have been privileged to train and to function as your humble servant leaders. We are extremely proud of the dedicated and powerfully anointed men and women of God you have become—pastors, evangelists, teachers, and missionaries. "Buy the Truth and sell it not!" Continue to keep the main thing the main thing—prayer and God's Word. You truly are the light of Jesus before this dark world.

By the Spirit of the Living God

…Not by might, nor by power, but by my spirit, says the Lord of hosts.

Zechariah 4:6

Everyone at times, faces challenges much too great for their own resources and abilities. Our greatest victories will not be won by our power and might. They will be won by God's power, which is far greater than our weakness and deficiency. Rather than trusting in ourselves and our talents, insight, and strength, we should put our confidence and trust in Jesus Christ and His great power!

If we are struggling and trying to make something happen and are in need of a breakthrough in our relationships, finances, job, or spiritual walk, we should do all we can in the natural to prepare the best we can to prepare for success. Yet, we must realize that true victory and prosperity comes only by the Spirit of Almighty God! When the Spirit of God flows over our soul and what we are trying to accomplish, we know the time is right to act, for we sense His anointing empowering us to achieve what we could not in our own power.

The breath of Jesus is blowing upon us today. This is our time! He will provide opportunities which no one can deny us. He is working in the background turning the situation in our favor. Let faith arise in knowing that God's stored-up blessings are about to be poured out to us!

Let us ask Jesus to forgive us for being overwhelmed and fearful due to obstacles, challenges, and opportunities placed before us. Then, surrender each area of our heart, mind, will, and emotions to Him. By His Holy Spirit, may He stir us to trust that his power is at work in us. Praise Him for directing our steps and for giving us the power to be overcomers in this life!

The Law of God in our Hearts

Which show the work of the law written in their hearts, their conscience also bearing witness, and their thoughts the mean while accusing or else excusing one another.

Romans 2:15

God had Moses to write His commandments on stone tablets for the children of Israel in the Old Testament. Now, since the beginning of the New Testament era, the law is written on our hearts, because Christ dwells within us as temples of the Holy Ghost!

Our very conscience sensitizes us to immediately recognize right from wrong and to know what we should do in order to please Jesus. The Spirit of the Lord within gives us the unction or prod to follow His will and to align our hearts and lives with His Word. Each time we are obedient to following scriptural principle and doing His will, we become sharper and more attuned to His direction and stronger in Him. Yet, if we continually override His guidance, we gradually become insensitive and hardened so that we are unable to distinguish His voice.

Let us determine to follow the Spirit's inner promptings, which will always lead us toward truth and righteousness. We draw nearer to Jesus each time we obey His promptings. His law and promises are written in our hearts to make it easier for us to always have access to Him and to make it safely through this dark world we live in.

Praise the Lord for abiding in us! His home in in us! We are the temple of the Holy Ghost! May we read, meditate on, and obey the Word, so we honor Jesus in everything we say and do.

Perfect Gifts from a Perfect God

Every good gift and every perfect gift is from above, and comes down from the Father of lights, with whom is no variableness, neither shadow of turning.

James 1:17

Jesus does not waver! He is dependable and, in His dependability, He gives good gifts! He created the Earth, the fullness thereof is His, and He has provided it for us to use. Every good gift and blessing in our lives begins on the spiritual level with God.

Jesus is a good God, and He desires to give good gifts to His children! He wants to supply all our needs according to His riches in glory, so that whatever we do will prosper. Jesus wants us to be filled with His Spirit so we will live joyfully and be wise and strong in our relationship with Him. We cannot even begin to imagine all the abundant blessings our God has in store for us (see I Corinthians 2:9).

Each gift provided to us is intended to draw us nearer to Jesus. He is the faithful and true rewarder of all that seek Him diligently (see Hebrews 11:6). Let us have faith to receive the blessings He has prepared us today. We should praise and thank Him for consistently giving us His grace, gifts, love, and for every promise in His Word. Nothing nor anyone compares to Jesus! No one cares for us like Him!

May Jesus open our eyes to His goodness and His perfect gifts. May He draw us near to Him and fill us with love, joy, and peace as we follow Him all the days of our life.

The Good Fight

Fight the good fight of faith, lay hold on eternal life, whereunto you are also called, and have professed a good profession before many witnesses.

I Timothy 6:12

The Christian life often involves difficult struggles that contains numerous pitfalls, which today's verse describes as a good fight. It is a fight in which we unite with Jesus against our common enemy. It is a spiritual battle where we stand firm on the truth of His Word and fight against the world, the flesh, the devil, and our own carnal will. Fighting this good fight of faith requires us to arise to the challenges of living the Christian life and to confidently embrace the calling and commission to do God's will on Earth.

The great news for us is that the battle has already been won by our Lord's victory on the cross. Because of what Jesus has done for us, we can face all life's battles by holding to an unwavering faith in Him, trusting Him to bring us through victoriously. Fighting the good fight of faith means we trust Him in all things and in so doing we are taking hold of eternal life. Eternal life does not only involve living forever in the life to come. It also involves living triumphantly in the present. We do this by growing in the knowledge and power of Jesus, and forming a deep intimacy with Him.

Our life is a testimony of His faithfulness, as we run the race that is set before us with patient endurance and a resolve to do God's will. May we fight the good fight of faith, knowing that the victory over the world, the flesh, and the devil, has already been won by Jesus. May we face the challenges of life with His strength and to His glory!

Jesus Our Avenger

And shall not God avenge his own elect, which cry day and night unto him, though he bear long with them?

Luke 18:7

If we have an overwhelming circumstance in our lives today that we have been crying out to Jesus for, a situation where we cannot seem to see any way out, there is hope in God. Our Lord is faithful to His Word and will always be faithful to keep His promises to us!

God is our avenger. He will fight on our behalf against our enemy's attacks. Our real warfare is not with people who offend us. Our real enemy is Satan, the devil who goes about as a roaring lion seeking whom he may devour. But rest assured, Jesus has a plan in place for our victory. He will in due time correct all the wrongs that have been committed against us.

Our responsibility is to surrender the situation to Jesus. We need not to become embroiled in a long discourse with those who attack us, attempting to straighten everything out. We know and trust that our God is fighting on our behalf to turn the enemies attempts to destroy us into blessings and favor.

We are often oppressed and tempted to be revengeful, but God says, "Vengeance is mine, I will repay." Remember we are the objects of His love. Even when people oppress us, we know assuredly that Jesus will defend us. Let us take our case to Jesus, lay the entire matter before Him, plead with Him, and then have confident assurance that He will intervene.

Today, we release every care, concern, and situation that is beyond our control to Jesus. We believe that Jesus is working things out for our good. He will tread all our enemies under His feet shortly. He is able to avenge us, and His Word is true.

Time to Use Our Gifts

Having then gifts differing according to the grace that is given to us…

Romans 12:6

Jesus has given us gifts and the power to use those gifts to accomplish good in the world. We are not judged by the type of gifts we have been given, but rather on whether and how we use them. Regardless of our gifts, God expects us to use them!

Jesus said, "My yoke is easy and my burden is light" (Matthew 11:30). This implies that we will sense peace and contentment when we operate in our gifts and callings. We will still face resistance and challenges anytime we do His will, yet we will have supernatural empowerment to accomplish our purpose. Living life in God's divine will and using what He has given us for good flows instinctively. If things we attempt always seem burdensome and exhausting, we may need to seek the Lord earnestly to determine if this is truly what He has called us to. We just know that we know, that we know when it is of God. We experience empowerment and refreshing in our soul as we operate in our calling.

We may be guilty of wasting valuable time wishing we were better at using our gifts or wishing we had different gifts rather than diligently using them the way Jesus intended. May today's verse convict us of the need to use the gifts we have been given. May God give us confidence to recognize our gifts so that we can use them effectively for His glory. Praise Him for empowering us to live by His grace.

Patiently Waiting on God's Promotion

For promotion comes neither from the east, nor from the west, nor from the south. But God is the judge: he puts down one, and sets up another.

Psalm 75:6-7

Jesus is in the business of building character in His children, therefore promotion in His kingdom does not come from our own man-made efforts. He puts down one and raises another. Authentic promotion is coordinated by Him.

Promotion comes as we flourish in the place God has planted us and when our character has formed properly and evidenced to be steady and consistent. One way the Lord determines if we are ready for advancement is through patience, as we develop spiritual maturity during the process of waiting for a fulfilled promise. As we wait patiently, Jesus deepens our life-message through the experience, which also provides us with valuable wisdom to share with others.

Remember, promotion comes from the Lord! If we will remain faithful and maintain a good attitude, God will promote us in spite of any obstacles attempting to hinder. A simple touch of His favor can suddenly turn things around in our lives!

Continue to endure. Remain faithful. Stay focused on doing good. Jesus will promote us at just the right time. Let us humbly submit ourselves to Him, for our God is good and faithful. He will not fail us. May we persistently align our work and life to scriptural principle and love and honor Jesus. Receive His mercy and grace today so we can live our lives pleasing to Him in all things.

Equipped by the Inspired Word of God

All scripture is given by inspiration of God, and is profitable for doctrine, for reproof, for correction, for instruction in righteousness: That the man of God may be perfect, thoroughly furnished unto all good works.

II Timothy 3:16-17

Jesus has equipped us with all that we need to fulfill our divine purpose and calling though His everlasting Word. He has anointed us through His Spirit, giving us the strength and capability to accomplish His will in our lives. Since Scripture is produced and formed by the very breath of God, each time we read, study, or meditate on the Word we receive greater anointing, increase our faith, and prepare ourselves for His work.

If we ever start to doubt whether we can do what Jesus wants us to do, we simply need to begin hiding His Word in our hearts more to strengthen our faith and to experience calm assurance. We are well able to fulfill our goals and to use our talents and ingenuity to achieve success in life. We can conquer any storm and overcome all obstacles in our path. Greater is He that is in us than all forces against us in the world! "What shall we then say to these things? If God be for us, who can be against us?" (Romans 8:31).

Today, stay focused on Scripture and the plan Jesus has for us. Refuse to become complacent or feeling mentally or emotionally defeated. Instead, know that we are God's anointed! We can do all things thought Christ! The Lord who has begun this great work in us will perform it! We believe it in the name of Jesus!

God's Grace is More than Enough

My grace is sufficient for thee, for my strength is made perfect in weakness....

II Corinthians 12:9

We each have days in which we feel weak or overwhelmed. Yet, Jesus has given us grace and power to carry us through troubling times and to move us onward to victory.

Jesus wants us to learn that His gracious strength and mercy are enough to sustain us, even in the midst of life's trials. Learning this lesson can be daunting. If we are to become like Jesus, then we must let go of our requirements on how God answers and open our hearts to His work to redeem others through us, regardless of the personal cost. Only then can we truly realize that his grace is sufficient for us!

The word "sufficient" means competent, enough, or skilled. We always have what we need by God's grace! We will never face anything that His grace cannot provide the strength we need to overcome. Jesus is more than enough! At times when we feel we cannot carry own, He will carry us with His grace to His oasis of love, where He restores and refreshes our soul. All the strength, joy, love, and peace we will ever need is in Him!

Regardless of what challenges we are facing, we are not facing them alone. We are never without hope, we are never without resources, and we are never without solutions, for God's grace is sufficient for us! His grace is all we need to be prepared to keep pressing forward into His victory.

Rest in Jesus

Come unto me, all you who labor and are heavy laden, and I will give you rest. Take my yoke upon you, and learn of me; for I am meek and lowly in heart: and you shall find rest unto your souls.

Matthew 11:29

Jesus said for us to rest. That sounds really great, doesn't it? In a world filled with busyness and constant activity, most of us could really use a little more rest. However, God's definition of rest may not be necessarily what we envision. With Him, there is a difference between doing nothing and resting, and a difference between feeling burdened and doing strenuous tasks. His call to come unto Him is not escapism.

Pursuing things for our own gratification leaves us exhausted and drained. Jesus promises to give us rest as we surrender to Him and take on His yoke and discipline our lives to His guiding Word. He will refresh and renew our strength while we take up our cross to follow Him, Jesus wants us to live a life of rest and peace. We can only realize it by walking in His divine purpose and will for our lives.

May we ask Jesus to forgive us for the many times we have tried to do everything in our own strength and endure on false rest. Let us place our life in His loving care and honor Him. Today, we should cast our cares on Jesus, surrender all to Him. When we release our burdens and follow Him, we will discover rest for our soul and peace in our heart.

Wonderful Peace in a Fallen World

*Peace I leave with you, my peace I give unto you: not as the world gives,
give I unto you. Let not your heart be troubled, neither let it be afraid.*

John 14:27

Countless people today are searching for real peace. They
search for it in relationships, activities, money, habits,
religion, and among other things. Genuine peace can only be
realized though a personal relationship with Jesus Christ. Only
Jesus can quench the thirsting and satisfy the longing of our
soul.

God's peace is not an absence of problems, strife, or the
end of all conflicts. This utopia will never be realized in a fallen
world. Yet, the divine presence of His Spirit can provide peace
in our difficulties. The Holy Spirit is within us to guide,
strengthen, encourage, comfort, refresh, and bless us with
peace which passes all understanding. We are never alone in
life's struggles, for Jesus is not simply with us, His presence is
in us!

Jesus wants to freely give us His peace. His peace is not as
the world's peace. It cannot be earned or bought. Everlasting
peace begins when we invite Jesus to be the Lord and Savior
over every area of our lives. As we align our will and our
thoughts, attitudes, and actions with God's Word, His peace,
which passes all understanding will overflow in our heart and
soul. Sensing true peace helps us to know that we are living in
His will and following His purpose for us, because He always
guides us to peace.

May Jesus give us a deeper appreciation of His abiding
presence within us and guide us by His Spirit to know Him
more intimately. May He help us by His Spirit to perform His
work more joyfully. Let us praise Him now for the gift of peace
that passes all understanding in our lives.

Unwavering Faith

And being not weak in faith, he considered not his own body now dead, when he was about a hundred years old, neither yet the deadness of Sarah's womb: He staggered not at the promise of God through unbelief; but was strong in faith, giving glory to God; And being fully persuaded that, what he had promised, he was able also to perform.

Romans 4:19-21

Abraham is regarded as our father in the faith. God had promised him that he would become the father of many nations, when it seemed impossible for him and Sarah, his wife, to have a child. He was a hundred years old when the promise was fulfilled. Today's passage tells us that Abraham did not consider the limitations of his own body nor Sarah's dead womb, which was humanly impossible to produce children. Rather than dwelling on all the adverse reasons he would not be able to have children, Abraham simply trusted God's ability to do anything and to perform what He had promised. Amazingly, "He staggered not at the promise of God through unbelief!"

Are we trusting Jesus today for the impossible? Have we been waiting and travailing in prayer seemingly far too long. Consider our God and His faithful promised Word! Impossibilities with people are opportunities with Him! Just as Abraham allowed God's promise to encourage and strengthen him, we must keep the faith—keep hoping, trusting, and believing. Our faith will guide us to victory in every situation! Jesus is well able to make a way even where there seems to be no way. He knows those who love and serve Him faithfully. Our faith can strengthen us just as Abraham's faith did for Him. Even if our circumstances seem impossible, praise and glorify God anyway. Our faith will move God to work powerfully on our behalf.

Jesus is the God who gives life to the dead and calls into existence the things that do not exist. May we possess the faith of Abraham, trusting fully in God's promise without wavering. Today, let us offer ourselves in faith to Jesus. Praise and thank Him for His faithfulness and strength at work in our lives. Set our minds on Him over any circumstances. Choose to trust Him and receive His strength. We give Jesus all the praise, honor, and glory forever, for He has done great things and will continue to do even greater things!

Awaiting the Perfect Day of Harvest

But the path of the just is as the shining light, that shines more and more unto the perfect day.

Proverbs 4:18

Truth and godliness in this verse compare to bright, straight, safe roads. Following godly wisdom is like walking on a road lit by light of dawn, brighter and brighter until it bursts into full day.

The Lord has appointed seasons in our lives in which we walk through challenging situations. When our expectations are not happening on our timetable, we can easily become frustrated. However, we should not allow a wrong attitude to prevent us from pressing onward.

We should understand that not all seasons are harvest seasons with Jesus. Before we reap the fruit of our labor, we have seasons in which we must plow, plant, water, and cultivate. Life would be simpler and easier if all seasons were times of increase and blessings. Yet, without the other seasons, we would be unprepared, and the harvest would produce little to nothing. During the hard season of plowing, the Lord brings to light and uproots areas of our life that we need to deal with. Before we can move to a new level, these must first be resolved.

Even if we are not progressing as rapidly as we would like, let us maintain an attitude of gratitude and confident expectation. During difficult times, keep plowing! Read, meditate upon, and apply Scripture to our lives daily, and speak words of life and faith! "And let us not be weary in welldoing: for in due season we shall reap, if we faint not" (Galatians 6:9). Our due season of harvest is on the way if we will remain faithful to God.

Praise Jesus today for His faithfulness to us in every season of our lives. Let us submit our ways to Him and trust Him to have the best plan for us. May we always walk in the light, so others can see our good works and glorify our Heavenly Father.

Fix Our Eyes on Jesus

Wherefore seeing we also are compassed about with so great a cloud of witnesses, let us lay aside every weight, and the sin which does so easily beset us, and let us run with patience the race that is set before us. Looking unto Jesus the author and finisher of our faith…

Hebrews 12:1-2

We We are surrounded by a great cloud of witnesses. Christians who have gone on before are testifying witnesses to the effect that we should lay aside every weight and anything that could hinder us from someday reaching our heavenly home. Their lives say to us, "Keep your eyes on Jesus, no matter what!"

The key to persistent godly living is fixing our eyes on Jesus. He is the author and finisher of our faith! We are complete in Him and He is the perfecter of our faith. He laid aside everything in order to come to this earth as a man so we could be free from any and all sin. We are to fix our eyes only upon Jesus because He can do what the other witnesses cannot do. They may inspire us and teach us valuable lessons, yet Jesus empowers us to live a victorious Christian life.

Jesus dwells within His faithful believers. In Him we have everything we need to win the race and to face life's challenges. He is our living Lord, ready to make available to us all that we need anytime we need it. The heavenly host is cheering us on today, saying, "You can make it! No weapon formed against you shall prosper! You are well able! You can win the race!" We can do all things through Christ Jesus!

Our Cup Overflows

...I have come that they may have life, and that they may have it more abundantly.

John 10:10

J esus does not want us stressing through life trying to merely survive. He desires for us to thrive, living an abundant and overflowing life.

During challenging times, we readily become locked in a survival mentality. However, if we focus only on survival, we may miss opportunities for advancement and future growth that Jesus has in store for us. He wants us to continue progressing to new levels and to trust Him for even greater in our lives. No matter what is happening in the world currently, His favor and blessing awaits for those who love and believe in Him.

May we determine to thrive daily, regardless of life's challenges. God's promises are true. Praise Him for abundant life! May Jesus give us a fresh realization of the overwhelming abundance He provides. Truly, our cup overflows.

The Chosen

According as he has chosen us in him before the foundation of the world,
that we should be holy and without blame before him in love.

Ephesians 1:4

Jesus wants us to be His holy children. That has been His intention for us before we were born and even before He created the world. He chose us!

Jesus called and chose us as His own children. We may have been rejected by others, denied promotion, or had our opinions ignored, yet God never fails to notice us. We are the apple of His eye. He has chosen us to "be holy and without blame before Him in love."

Let us ponder this truth today. Jesus values us above everything else He has created. We are special to Him and He loves us with an everlasting love. He knows everything about us and even knows the number of hairs on our head. He loves us so much that He came to this earth, died on a cross, and rose again to save us from our sins. Always remember the value He has placed in us. We have been chosen by God and nothing can alter His love for us!

What an amazing honor we have to be one of God's adopted children. May we bring continuous joy to Him in the way we live. May He forgive us for the times we have disappointed Him or not lived up to what He desires of us. May our life be a holy thanksgiving to Jesus. Let us praise Him daily for loving us!

Closer Than the Air We Breathe

Have not I commanded you? Be strong and of a good courage; be not afraid, neither be dismayed: for the Lord your God is with you whithersoever you go.

Joshua 1:9

Jesus will never leave nor desert us! Be strong, for our Lord is always near, even if it does not seem like it. Everywhere we go His presence is close and within. We are never alone. We never have to fear. Not even death can separate us from His love!

Regardless of what we deal with today in our lives, we can face the day with courage and boldness, for Jesus is with us and He supplies our every need. He is our provider, our shepherd, our healer, our righteousness, our sanctifier, and our constant source of wisdom, strength, love, peace, and joy! We are assured that our physical, spiritual, and emotional needs will be supplied, because Jesus is with us!

Let us open our hearts and believe to receive all we need today. May we start by praising Jesus for His provision in our lives and press onward with confident expectancy, realizing our Lord goes with us through everything. May our God be near, not only in His promise and in His presence, but also in our awareness. We should realize He is always near. May He give us courage to deal with the endless challenges we face by empowering us with His strength and unfailing love. Jesus is closer than the air we breathe.

Encourage One Another

Wherefore comfort yourselves together, and edify one another, even as also you do.

I Thessalonians 5:11

In a world where we are continuously pressured to accept new philosophies and trends, as Christians, we need to comfort and encourage one another in faith for holding the line on truth and righteousness. Novel things are not usually godly things. This is why God tells us to search for the old paths of Scriptural principles and to walk therein.

Jesus has designed us to live in relationship with others. We are to help one another grow in the Lord and in life. We cannot achieve our greatest potential alone. We reach our fullest potential by having those in our lives who will teach and encourage us toward excellence. God wants us to do the same for others.

"Encourage" means "to inspire with hope, courage or confidence, and to give support to." We can recognize talents and strengths in others that they may be unaware of themselves. They may not see what we see in them. They need our encouragement and for us to show that we believe in them. We may choose to do this with compliments, by sending them a special note or gift, or possibly by taking time to work with them. If we help others achieve their goals, the Lord will help us achieve ours as well. As we pour into others, Jesus pours into us. "Give and it shall be given unto you…" (Luke 6:38).

Let us thank God for placing people in our life. May we do those things that are pleasing to Jesus and may He grant us the wisdom and motivation to encourage and strengthen them for His glory.

Choose Jesus by Choosing Forgiveness

…But if any has caused grief, … you ought rather to forgive him, and comfort him, lest perhaps such an one should be swallowed up with overmuch sorrow.

2 Corinthians 2:5 & 7

We all have people in our lives who have offended and wronged us in some way. They may have done this intentionally, or possibly, they may not even realize what they did to hurt us so. Regardless of the details, as Christians, we should forgive them.

We are called by Jesus to forgive, because He has forgiven us. We discover God through love when we forgive, for God is love. Anytime we do not choose love and forgiveness, we go in the reverse direction, farther away from the Lord.

We do not excuse bad actions when we choose to forgive. We simply let go of our offender's debt to us, so Jesus can release our debt owed to Him. Forgiving others, frees us from spiritual, mental, and emotional bondage. Furthermore, it releases God's favor to provide ample opportunities for us to advance to new levels in each area of our lives.

May God heal the wounds of our heart, as we determine this day to forgive anyone who may have offended us. By seeking love and forgiveness, we choose Jesus! We become more like Him every time we forgive

Whosoever Believes

For God so loved the world, that he gave his only begotten Son, that whosoever believes in him should not perish, but have everlasting life.

Psalm 5:3

God loves us! That is the great and victorious message of the Bible. That is the most wonderful news we could ever receive. God came to earth as a babe in a manger to show how much He loves us. "Greater love hath no man than this, that a man lay down his life for his friends" (John 15:13).

Jesus gave His life, so we could have life. He truly loves us unconditionally! Because of what He has done, anyone who believes on Him can experience salvation and receive everlasting life. Anyone can become His child. The blood of Jesus cleanses us from all sin! How amazing is this? We become the temple of God, where He abides continuously within.

We cannot fully understand the love Jesus has for us. "Oh, love of God, how rich and pure! How measureless and strong!" (Fredrick Leman). However, we should daily thank and praise Him with all of our heart. May He forgive us for the times our life has not reflected His loving appraisal of our value. May we believe Him enough to accept what He says about us and what He has done for us. Let us surrender our full trust in His love, so He will continue His transformational work of redemption in us.

Let us praise Jesus for making us better. Thank him for saving us from our sin and for giving us life with Him. We are free indeed because of His great love!

Walk in Love

It is an honor for a man to cease from strife….

Proverbs 20:3

Strife can be a very destructive force to relationships. It usually starts small and escalates much worse as pride joins in. We behave honorably and honor the Lord when we determine to walk in love, cease from strife, and forgive offenses.

We can avoid strife by loving people and valuing our relationship with them over our selfish desires or pride. We conquer strife through love. Love covers a multitude of sins and offenses. Love tries to understand from others' perspective and readily forgives. If individuals in our lives have been unfriendly or curt with us at home or work, rather than becoming upset, choose to respond in love by being patient and kind toward them. They could have misplaced aggression toward us due to problems of which we may be unaware.

Anyone can start a fight or argument, but when we walk in the love of Jesus, we are able to control our emotions and speak the things that please Him. When we refuse to repay evil with evil, insult with insult, or spite with spite, we essentially demonstrate greater spiritual maturity. We earn respect from others by walking in love. Love refuses to let an issue fester and seeks to avoid disputes before they even begin.

Today, let us not allow ourselves to be drawn into petty arguments. Stop them before they can start. Even if we do become upset or angry, choose never to go to bed angry. Determine to resolve all disputes quickly so that they do not develop into catastrophes. Walking in love is satisfying and wonderful and we praise Jesus for empowering us to do it!

Peace Within

Peace I leave with you, my peace I give unto you: not as the world gives, give I unto you. Let not your heart be troubled, neither let it be afraid.

John 14:27

Having peace with Jesus is not the absence of problems. All difficulties will not end in this world as we currently know it. Jesus grants us the gift of His Holy Spirit to guide us through all our troubles, so that we may supernaturally experience peace as we face life's storms and struggles in this fallen world.

Christ is present within to lead, strengthen, comfort, encourage, motivate, bless, and to supply all our needs. We are never alone through any challenges, for Jesus is with us. We also have Christ within—our Prince of Peace, Mighty God, Wonderful, Counselor, and Everlasting Father!

Regardless of what may be happening in our lives today, we can still have peace in our heart, mind, and soul. We must never allow negative experiences to take away our peace. "For God hath not given us the spirit of fear; but of power, and of love, and of a sound mind" (2 Timothy 1:7).

The peace of God grants us amazing power to think clearly, to hear His voice, to make wise decisions, and even promotes better health for our mind and body. Refuse to let anything steal our peace today. Choose to receive the peace of God which surpasses all understanding. When we live in divine peace, nothing the enemy throws at us can defeat us!

Renewed Hope and Joy

To appoint unto them that mourn in Zion, to give unto them…the garment of praise for the spirit of heaviness; that they may be called trees of righteousness, the planting of the Lord, that he may be glorified.

Isaiah 61:3

God wants us to wear a new garment! He is not referring to physical attire, rather He refers to what is covering our mind, heart, and emotions.

Many are currently clothed with hopelessness and discouragement. Their wearing a depleting spirit of heaviness. This may have resulted from painful experiences or circumstances with family, friends, or co-workers. Scripture tells us there is "A time to weep, and a time to laugh; a time to mourn, and a time to dance" (Ecclesiastes 3:4). It is time for us to let go of all our hurt and release it to Jesus, and He will replace it with a garment of praise.

If the heaviness of our past is weighing us down and preventing us from moving forward, it is time for a new garment of praise! Our new garment's material is much lighter, for it is made of peace, joy, and love that is manufactured by God Himself. He owns all the creative copyrights to it and wants to freely share it with us.

Lay all those heavy burdens down today by forgiving any who have offended us and begin basking in glorious adoration and praise to our Mighty God! Praise Him for new life, opportunity, people who genuine care about us, and for His blessing and favor each day! Let us thank Him for restoring our joy, peace, and love, so we "might be called trees of righteousness, the planting of the Lord, that he might be glorified."

Get Ready for Our Minds to Be Blown!

Now unto him that is able to do exceedingly abundantly above all that we ask or think, according to the power that works in us, Unto him be glory in the church by Christ Jesus throughout all ages, world without end. Amen.

Ephesians 3:20-21

Jesus has done so much for us that sometimes all we have left to do is to simply praise and glorify Him for all the wonderful things He has done! Although we have natural talents and abilities, we could have never come this far without His favor and blessing over us. Our God is able to do exceedingly abundantly above all we can imagine! Hallelujah!

I Corinthians 2:9 tells us that "Eye hath not seen, nor ear heard, neither have entered into the heart of man, the things which God hath prepared for them that love him." God's Spirit works in us by faith as we trust and believe that He is able. He desires for His blessings to overtake us and to blow our minds by how great and wonderful He is! If we have but mustard seed faith today, the smallest seed of faith, we can see the Lord move insurmountable obstacles and mountains on our behalf.

Our faith continues to grow as we hear, read, study, and meditate on Scripture, for faith comes by hearing and hearing by God's Word. Let us prioritize our commitment to the Holy Scriptures of the Bible. As we do this, our faith will grow, and we will realize that Jesus will do exceedingly abundantly above all we can ask or think. Our God is faithful to keep every promise to us which He has given in His Word. May our daily life bring glory to the mighty name of Jesus.

Our Mighty Deliverer

Many are the afflictions of the righteous: but the Lord delivers him out of them all.

Psalm 34:19

Although the righteous have difficulties, we realize that our God delivers us from them all! All that happens to us will eventually result in our deliverance, whether through our death to be with God eternally or whether through our freedom from oppression in order to continue our work for Jesus (see Philippians 1:19-23). Our deliverance is secure!

We are conquerors in Christ Jesus. Nothing can separate us from God's love, not even death. Even if we are currently feeling afflicted or burdened by the cares of life, our God is working to deliver us and to make us better. He may not use the method we expected, but we can trust that Jesus has our best interest in mind. Afflictions are only temporary. We may not feel like rejoicing, but if we will arise in praise and adoration to Jesus, we can expedite our deliverance, for He inhabits the praises of His people. He will empower us to prevail over all afflictions and shower us with His blessing and favor. May Jesus grant us the faith we need to believe that whatever happens in our lives will not pull us away from His love and deliverance for us. Jesus is a great and mighty Deliverer!

Following God's Path

But while he thought on these things, behold, the angel of the Lord appeared unto him in a dream, saying, Joseph, son of David, fear not to take unto you Mary your wife: for that which is conceived in her is of the Holy Ghost.

Matthew 1:20

We can only imagine how Joseph felt, who became engaged to Mary only to discover during the betrothal period she was pregnant. Had he made a mistake in choosing Mary? Things certainly did not turn out how He had planned. But God! But God sent an angel to assure Joseph that he was choosing the right direction by taking Mary to be his wife.

We sometimes feel anxious or overwhelmed by the calling Jesus has commissioned us to fulfill. We focus on our goals, yet circumstances do not always emerge as we had intended. Today, let us be encouraged in the Lord by trusting that He understands and is guiding us to the place where we need to be. Even if our current situation seems confusing and unsettling, Jesus is with us, and He will not fail. May we not be fearful, but may we trust that our God is working on our behalf to guide us into the storehouse of blessings He has awaiting us.

Let us praise Jesus for His perfect love which casts out all fear. May we love Him and surrender every area of our life to Him.

Be A Cheerful Giver

And when they were come into the house, they saw the young child with Mary his mother, and fell down, and worshipped him: and when they had opened their treasures, they presented unto him gifts; gold, and frankincense and myrrh.

Matthew 2:11

King Herod used the news of Jesus' birth in an attempt to kill Him. Yet, the wise men used this glorious news to search for and to worship the Lord. Their worship of Jesus consisted of their giving. They gave of themselves their time, possessions, love, devotion, and honor. When we sincerely come to worship Jesus, we will offer our time, treasure, love, honor, and ourselves. The Lord then discloses His will and shows us how to support His cause in the world.

The wise men were fully in awe at meeting Jesus. They fell to the ground worshipping Him with all they had to offer. Giving was an instinctive response. They freely gave to Him generously from their hearts all their love and the gifts they had brought. They gave from a heart of gratitude and from a desire to honor Him. Jesus expects us to give freely and generously from our hearts, because He gave His life for us without any reservation in order to save us from sin. "Every man according as he purposes in his heart, so let him give; not grudgingly, or of necessity: for God loves a cheerful giver" (II Corinthians 9:7). He wants us to be happy to give. God loves a cheerful giver!

Christmas is all about giving. Jesus gave until it hurt! "Give, and it shall be given unto you; good measure, pressed down, and shaken together, and running over, shall men give into your bosom" (Luke 6:38). What are we willing to do for Him who has done so much for us? Think about our blessings and God's faithfulness today and let our hearts overflow with praise and adoration of Him. Just as the wise men, giving will be an automatic response! May Jesus receive our heartfelt worship and praise and use us to advance his good news to the world.

Setting the Tone with Prayer

My voice shall you hear in the morning, O Lord; in the morning will I direct my prayer unto you, and will look up.

Psalm 5:3

Prayer is more than simply asking God for more, offering praise, and interceding for others. Prayer is expecting and realizing that Jesus wants us to spend time in His presence. Prayer is believing God hears and He will respond to what we trust Him for and He will empower us to be who He wants us to be.

In prayer, we eagerly anticipate that Jesus will meet us and do what is best for us and for those we love. Each morning we can set the tone for our entire day. By praying to Jesus and having a grateful heart and a positive mental attitude, we attract favor, blessing, and opportunity. We daily set our path for achievement and victory.

Let us start our day on the right path. Begin by praising the Lord and thanking Him for all He has done. Praise Him for meeting us in our prayer time. We know that He hears us and cares about what we share with Him. Thank Him for paying attention to someone like each of us and accepting us as His precious children. Finally, praise Him for His goodness and mercy and for paving our way to success and victory!

Prepare the Way

The voice of him that cries in the wilderness, Prepare the way of the Lord,
make straight in the desert a highway for our God.

Isaiah 40:3

Today's verse tells us to prepare. Each of us experience times of waiting, yet some individuals expect to wait for God to do everything without any effort from them personally. We must do our part and prepare. Jesus is returning for a bride (church) who has made herself ready.

To prepare for what God wants to do, we should pray, be filled with the Holy Spirit, internalize Scripture, and discipline ourselves in obedience to the Word. The words from our mouth, the meditation of our heart, and our actions should be pleasing to the Lord.

David said, "My time is in your hand…" (Psalm 31:15). Jesus said, "It is not for you to know the times or the seasons, which the Father has put in his own power" (Acts 1:7). We may not know when nor how God will intervene on our behalf, yet we know He will work according to our ultimate good.

Let us remain steady and productive for the Lord and expect good things. Even if things do not happen the way we anticipate, may we not feel discouraged. Trust that regardless of what occurs, we are moving closer to realizing God's promises. Let us dedicate ourselves afresh to Jesus. May He show us how to prepare ourselves for all He has in store. "Prepare the way of the Lord!"

Put Wings On Our Faith

But wilt you know, O vain man, that faith without works is dead?

James 2:20

According to this verse, many people who claim to be believers appear to actually be spiritual corpses. When we have genuine faith, it will be verified in service. In addition to moving mountains, faith moves believers to act in ways that honor Jesus and blesses others.

If we have been waiting for Jesus to do great things in our lives, we should not passively wait. If we have invited friends to visit, we do not simply wait for them to show up to make things ready. We clean the house and prep the meals usually well in advance of their arrival. Similarly, as we await our Lord's promise and visitation, we should constantly work in making preparation for what He will do and do all we can to please Him from our heart of love and appreciation for Him. Works puts wings on our faith and opens doors for God to move mightily!

Today, let us ask Jesus to forgive us for the times we have been lazy in our spiritual walk. May He open our spiritual eyes to see the many opportunities for service He avails us daily. May He also empower us to put our faith into action in these opportunities in ways that blesses others. Please Jesus, teach us to wait correctly.

Heavenly Perspective

Set your affection on things above, not on things on the earth.

Colossians 3:2

We are called to set our heart and mind on the realities of heaven. We should keep our focus on things above and trust in Jesus over our limited abilities., rather than being influenced by the things of the world. We find our sufficiency in Christ Jesus, for we have a heavenly inheritance awaiting us which can never perish nor fade away.

We will never rise to new levels or fulfill our God-given destiny by focusing in the natural realm. We must set our hearts and minds higher, on the things above, to develop the right perspective. Focusing on the carnal worldview allows fear and circumstances to hinder our progress. However, when we walk by faith and not by sight, we believe before we see, and we begin to see the way Jesus sees. "Through faith we understand that the worlds were framed by the word of God, so that things which are seen were not made of things which do appear" (Hebrews 11:3).

Let us set our hearts and minds on things above today and focus on all the goodness Jesus has in store. Shut out all negativity, fear, and doubt. Allow ourselves to hear the inner voice of the Holy Spirit leading us in the way we should go. May we keep the eyes of our heart on Jesus and the glorious eternal inheritance that He has reserved for us!

Perfected Strength

And he said unto me, My grace is sufficient for you: for my strength is made perfect in weakness...

II Corinthians 12:9

When we pray, we sometimes find ourselves expecting Jesus to do what we want, rather than what is best or most beneficial for us and for Him. Paul learned that the Lord's strength and mercy were more than enough to sustain him through every struggle. God desires for us to learn a similar lesson. True followers of Jesus will go through difficulties, yet His grace is sufficient, and His strength is perfect.

If we are to become like Jesus, we must release our requirements on God's answers to our prayers and accept His work to redeem others through us, in spite of our personal cost. Only then will we really know that His grace is sufficient for us! Our God is greater than any struggle we face! He can take our struggles and use them to strengthen us, but we must do our part by taking steps of faith toward the victory. To become free from the bondages we are in, we must do something. We must pray, believe, and press through to victory.

Regardless of what we may be facing today, remember God's grace is sufficient for us. May He guard our heart from discouragement in difficult times and guard it from arrogance in good times. Let us praise Jesus for giving us a permanent, steadfast hope of Heaven. His strength is made perfect in us. He has given us everything we need to overcome in this life! Let us put our trust in Him and declare that He is good and faithful. Jesus is equipping us for victory in every area of our lives.

Restoration

The thief comes not, but for to steal, and to kill, and to destroy: I have come that they may have life, and that they may have it more abundantly.

John 10:10

Sometimes, our lives consist of just trying to survive and make it through the day. With the constant pressures of the world and satanic forces working against us, it can be difficult to hold on to our vision. Jesus did not come to us and sacrifice His life on a cross so we could merely survive. He wants us to receive His love and empowerment of His Holy Spirit so we can thrive and live a more abundant life!

Let us step out on faith and declare, "Today is my turn around! I'm coming out of this funk of simply hoping nothing else bad is going to happen. I choose to live in joy and victory of God's power and love! I am a child of the King of kings and Lord of lords!" Jesus is ready to open the windows of Heaven and allow each of us to begin a new season of restoration of joy, love, and peace; and not only this, He wants to restore relationships and heal broken hearts and bruised souls. Hard times do not last forever, but God's Word and promises abide forever. He will do what He has promised to do. He chose us in Him to not merely survive, but to thrive!

Something good is about to happen in our lives! Jesus is passing by! Reach out and touch Him and we will never be the same!

Joy is Knocking

For his anger endures but a moment; in his favor is life: weeping may endure for a night, but joy comes in the morning.

Psalm 30:5

Jesus is the God of all comfort. Our ultimate good is intended, even when He deals harshly with our sin and rebellion. His chastening lasts for a short time and then He restores the joy of our salvation. For those who may have sinned and are dealing with its consequences, do not lose heart. A new day will dawn with God's amazing grace and mercy.

As we awake to a new day and even a new year, God wants to give us joy. Let us arise in faith and determine that this is going to be a wonderful day and the beginning of a fresh and glorious year! The joy of the Lord has arrived at our doorstep. All we need to do is open the door and allow it into our lives. The joy of the Lord is our strength and in His presence is fullness of Joy.

Let us start each day by thanking Jesus for another beautiful day and for bringing us through many difficult circumstances. Choose to be happy and to enjoy every single day. May we also brighten others' days. Receive God's gift of joy! In Jesus name!

Take a Drink

But whosoever drinks of the water that I shall give him shall never thirst;
but the water that I shall give him shall be in him a well of water
springing up into everlasting life.

John 4:14

Jesus promises water which leads to everlasting life for the tired and thirsty soul! The living water of His Spirit dwelling within us lasts forever!

Too often, we settle for facade rather than substance. Only Jesus can supply what our thirsty souls long for. Only He can fill the emptiness and the longing in our hearts. Jesus offers refreshing spring water, which will never become stagnant. The living water He fills us with is the Holy Spirit. He cleanses and transforms our lives by His very presence. Only Jesus can quench our soul's thirst.

Today, we all might have things to come against us spiritually. We may feel the heat and pressure from our circumstances trying to upset us or cause us stress. Take time for a fresh drink of Living Water, saying, "Jesus, I need you!" He will restore our peace and renew our strength.

Are we thirsty? Does our hungry and thirsty soul need to be filled? The dry spiritual desert of this world may have left us famished. We have tasted of God's goodness. We have drunk from His Fountain. We can turn to Jesus, receive from Him, and we will find rest and refreshing for our soul. Anytime, just take a drink!

Our Delight In God

Delight yourself also in the Lord: and he shall give you the desires of your heart.

Psalm 37:4

God is inviting us to seek a loving relationship with Him, rather than viewing this verse as a way to have our wish list filled. When we delight in Him, we discover our priorities properly align with His will and our hearts attune to know what is truly valuable and what is not. Our greatest desire should be to delight in Jesus.

We will go to great lengths to do what makes us happy. We will work long hours and expend all our energy to achieve our desired result. It is okay to enjoy our work and achievements, yet the Lord wants us to delight ourselves in Him. True joy can only be found in loving and serving Him. In addition to meaning "to give great pleasure," the word "delight" also means "to soften or to make pliable," like clay in the potter's hands. Jesus wants to mold us and make us into His image, so He can use us for His great work in the world. When we do this, we position ourselves for Him to grant us the desires of our heart!

Far too often, our hearts desire selfish things. Yet, today, let us take a few moments to realize that Jesus is what we need above all else and allow His will to be our heart's desire. May His Spirit be ignited within us, so we can recognize any selfish deception that has distracted us from putting Him first in our lives. Ask Jesus to forgive us for times we have been petty, selfish, and superficial. May we know Jesus more intimately and delight ourselves in His ways each day.

After This

And after this it came to pass that David smote the Philistines, and subdued them...

II Samuel 8:1

We may have experienced numerous setbacks, yet Jesus has an "after this" in store for us. Our victory is just around the bend. He will turn our setbacks into steppingstones to achieve greater spiritual maturity and to obtain new levels in every part of our lives. Our God desires to take us farther than we can possibly imagine!

During our difficult times, Satan tries to convince us that we will never be happy again, our best days have passed, and our setbacks have destroyed our future. Yet, God wants us to realize that restoration power is on the way. Keep holding on to Jesus because He is still holding on to us! After all the heartache, pain, and disappointments, a victorious and full life is in store. Our best days and ultimate joy are ahead of us.

Remain faithful to God and patient during the hard times. Resist becoming bitter or depressed. God has an "after this" awaiting. Jesus will not only lead us out to victory, but He will also make us even better than before! Our God is great! In times of pain, He gives power. In times of sickness, He provides healing and after a loss, He is the one who restores what was lost. On the other side of our pain is restoration and abundant joy!

Learn to Turn Away

It is an honor for a man to cease from strife: but every fool will be meddling.
Psalm 46:10

Satan tries various methods to distract us from pursuing our divine purpose and calling. These distractions may come from an easily offended family member, an unfriendly coworker, or an obnoxious neighbor. These situations can easily become magnified from our perspective, yet Jesus wants us to remain focused on eternal implications. We must not allow the small things to cause our life unnecessary conflict or stress.

In chapter 17 of the Book of Samuel, Eliab, David's oldest brother, tried to start an argument with David just before he was to battle the giant Goliath. David ignored his brother and remained focused on his mission. He knew disputing with Eliab was not worth his time or energy. He realized his real battle was with Goliath. Like David, we should determine not to allow petty people and trivial things to steal our attention from what is most important in life. We should simply turn away and remain focused on what we are called to do.

As Christians, we are to have nothing to do with strife because it is always caused by ungodly traits, like pride or jealousy, and it leads to arguments. We are to love others as ourselves, but strife does not do that. Let us remain fixated on the big picture of the important things in life today. May Jesus grant us wisdom to realize when we should avoid strife and receive honor from Him.

Choose Love

For where envying and strife is, there is confusion and every evil work.

James 3:16

Numerous times God's Word commands us to love. Love is the greatest force in the universe, for God is love. Nothing is more valuable or important on earth. Love is enduring and all that lasts eternally.

The Lord expects that we walk in love. Whenever we are envious, combative, or selfish, we invite confusion and every evil work into our lives. Yet, if we walk in love, the love of God shields us. We should determine to put Jesus first and decide to be patient and kind toward everyone. We disrupt our enemy's strategies against us and those we care about when we choose love!

Let us evaluate whether we are truly walking in love by using I Corinthians 13 as our guide. Humbly ask Jesus to search our hearts, to remove any selfishness, and to help us to walk in love. Love is not simply an emotion. Love is a decision. May the love of God be "shed abroad in our hearts today by the Holy Ghost which is given unto us" (I Corinthians 5:5), so we can experience His supernatural grace and security.

Look Up!

Set your affection on things above, not on things on the earth.

Colossians 3:2

Some days we do not feel as excited or energetic as other days. Yet, if we set our minds on things above, the joy and excitement of loving and serving Jesus arises within!

God has so much greater in store for us in the supernatural realm, so much more than the temporal things of this world can merely provide. What we set our hearts and minds on is what we will see manifested in our lives. Therefore, we should daily center our attention on God's goodness and keep our faith and hope alive.

Rather than looking for excuses of why we should be sad, let us cultivate the vision and dreams the Lord has given us. Determine not to feel discouraged or defeated. We may be facing difficulties, yet victory awaits us, IN JESUS NAME! Arise today expecting the good things Jesus has in store!

Choose Happiness

This is the day which the Lord has made; we will rejoice and be glad in it.

Psalm 118:24

Happiness is an attitude that we choose, not a circumstance that simply occurs in our lives. We often make excuses of why we feel unhappy. We are unhappy because of our relationships, our job, our weight, and we can easily think of numerous other excuses to remain unhappy. Today, let us determine to be happy now!

We can always find something to keep being unhappy, but this is not the life Jesus wants us to choose. We must rid ourselves of all excuses and decide to enjoy our life and God's blessing on us here and now! This is the day, today and right now, the Lord has made; we will rejoice and be glad in it! We refuse to wait until tomorrow, next week, next month, or next year for our happiness. Determine to honor Jesus immediately by deciding to enjoy Him and all He has done for us.

This is the day our Lord has made! Praise Jesus for this day and for another opportunity to glorify and honor Him with our life. Let us choose to be glad in Him every single moment!!

Capture the Little Foxes

Take us the foxes, the little foxes, that spoil the vines…

Song of Solomon 2:15

Hurricanes and tornadoes receive better news coverage, yet in the bigger scheme of things termites cause greater damage. The little things, rather than the big things, are usually what keep us from being happy and content with life. Today's verse reminds us that we do not daily face great crises—e.g., terminal illness, broken relationships, job loss, or financial crisis. The small aggravations and disruptions are usually what trigger our emotions and eat away at our peace and joy.

How we deal with the small things can define the type of life we live. If we fill our minds with negativity and constantly reflect on our inconveniences and difficulties, we allow the "little foxes" to "spoil the vines." They rob us of our energy and enjoyment. The word "take" in this verse means "to catch." By thinking positive thoughts about our blessings and God's goodness toward us, we capture the little foxes and establish the foundation for having a wonderful day.

Decide not to allow the little foxes to spoil our day by capturing every negative thought and attitude, before they can progress any farther. Let us determine to move onward and upward in joy and peace by meditating on Scripture and allowing God's Word to bring light and life to our emotions and our attitude. "This is the day which the Lord has made; we will rejoice and be glad in it" (Psalm 118:24).

Best Friends

Iron sharpens iron; so a man sharpens the countenance of his friend.

Proverbs 27:17

The best friends are those who help us draw nearer to Jesus! Real friends remain connected to us through the good times and the bad. They seldom get in our way unless we are going down. A true friend is not someone who simply agrees with everything we say or goes along with anything we want to do. Friends recognize our flaws, speak the truth, and love and care about us anyway.

Jesus does not bring individuals into our lives who we can shape to be just like us. He brings people to us having different personalities, interests, and strengths than ours. Because of the unique qualities everyone possesses, we can sharpen each other and cause one another to advance to new levels spiritually and in life. To enjoy the company of friends we must learn to appreciate their differences and be willing to learn from them. None of us are perfect. We may not be able to fix everyone, but we can love them. We frequently are amazed at how people work to improve areas in their lives, simply from being aware that someone loves and cares for them. God is not asking us to judge each other, but He is asking us to sharpen one another, so we can move ahead in His divine plan for our lives.

May we keep one another sharp and focused on building the kingdom of God. The way we see people is how we will treat them. May we see others as Jesus sees them and show gratitude for how we sharpen each other

The Treasure of Having Contentment

...I have learned, in whatsoever state I am, therewith to be content.

Philippians 4:11

One of the greatest treasures in life is to find contentment in godliness. When we discover this treasure, carnal situations and circumstances become less significant than the character we demonstrate in them. Loving Jesus with all our heart becomes most important. Life's goals become not how rich or powerful we can be, but how rich and powerful we are in God's grace and love!

We easily become focused on our dreams and desires, so much that they consume us, and our life becomes very imbalanced. We then associate our happiness to what we can acquire or achieve. Fear of losing people or things is a sure sign that we have established an idol in our heart. Genuine joy never comes from people or things. Jesus is the only source of real joy and contentment deep within. In His presence is fulness of joy and the joy of the Lord is our strength!

When we learn to be content despite our circumstances, we render Satan powerless over our lives. He no longer has the ability to discourage or frustrate us. Our level of contentment reveals our measure of faith in Jesus. Determine to trust Him in whatever state we are in! We will realize supernatural love, joy, peace, and blessings will overflow in our lives.

May Jesus still our restless and sometimes covetous hearts. May He help us experience contentment in His presence and character in life.

Setting the Stage

My voice shall you hear in the morning, O Lord; in the morning will I direct my prayer unto you, and will look up.

Psalm 5:3

In addition to making our requests to God in prayer, we give praise and thanksgiving, and even intercede on the behalf of others. Jesus listens intently anytime we pray and is ready to move life's mountains to help us. He wants to do what is best for us and for those we love. He is simply waiting for us to take time to sincerely pray.

David is described in Scripture as a man after God's own heart. He experienced the Lord working miraculous works all through his life. From today's verse, we realize that David set the stage for his day by praying and seeking the Lord each morning. Regardless of what he would face, divisions in his family, betrayal by friends, or powerful giants and enemies, his number one priority was to seek the Lord every morning.

Each day is a new day, with new opportunities and renewed hope! If we will spend time with Jesus and make Him our first and main priority, we will see Him work mightily for us too. Determine to seek Him first every morning, regardless of what is happening in our lives. By doing this, we will set the stage for a good and victorious day, in the name of Jesus!

Renewed Passion

Not slothful in business; fervent in spirit; serving the Lord.

Romans 12:11

Today's verse commands us to never be lazy, but to work hard and to serve Jesus enthusiastically and with passion. Sadly, many have lost their passion and enthusiasm for life. God wants us to return to our first love and passion for Him. Although we have endured numerous disappointments which may have stolen our fire, we can discover newness of life again!

We can easily become distracted by social media, watching news or movies, and spending time with friends or work, which results in us feeling detached from the things of God. We are to live our lives wholeheartedly for Jesus. We are to work hard and to serve Him enthusiastically. Serving God should not be something we fit in on Sunday if we have the time or unless we think we have something better to do. Loving and serving Jesus should be the way we live our lives.

Anything we allow to replace spending time with God tells us that something is out of place. Serving Jesus should be our number one priority…and we should enjoy it! It is a wonderful and enjoyable experience to bless someone in need, to read Scripture, and to worship God in praise and prayer. It is enjoyable trusting Jesus through difficult times and seeing Him work miracles in our lives.

Let us serve God wholeheartedly and enthusiastically. Our Lord never intended for us to be mediocre or stagnant. He is an extraordinary God, and we are to be a reflection of Him. Refuse to let the fire go out! Stay passionate about life and the divine purpose God has birthed on the inside of us! May Jesus rekindle and stir up the passion in our hearts, so we can stay on fire for Him.

Limitless God

I have seen an end of all perfection: but your commandment is exceedingly broad.

Psalm 119:96

There is no such thing as perfection in anything which is the work of humans, yet God's Word is broader than all our imperfections. Today's verse reveals a perfection which convicts us for shortcomings as well as for transgressions and does not allow us to make up for deficiencies in one direction by special carefulness in others. The path to freedom and perfection is only through the perfect one, Jesus Christ!

God's promises never return void. His Word stands true forever! If we will submit to His will and live according to His commandments, there is no limit to what He can do in our lives. Perfection is beyond our own ability to obtain. However, we must realize that we serve a supernatural God! If Jesus can make everything out of nothing, then He can certainly do exceedingly abundantly above all that we can imagine.

Today, may we shift our eyes and thoughts from this limited natural realm, and begin looking at God's supernatural realm, and focus on His unlimited possibilities for us and our future! We lift our eyes to Jesus! He alone is the source of our strength, peace, and provision. As limited creatures, how do we respond to our limitless, perfect God? May it be in worship and awe for the Jesus, whose infinite power is perfected in our weakness and whose overflowing grace is sufficient for our every need (II Corinthians 12:9). May we respond in gratitude for His measureless love for us that knows no bounds (Romans 8:39). And may we respond by delighting in obedience to keep His exceedingly broad commandment.

Through the Fire

*…We went through fire and through water: but you brought us out into a
wealthy place.*

Psalm 66:12

Too many Christians pray for Jesus to get them out of the
fire and the flood. Yet, believers should pray, "Lord, bring
us through the fire and flood, so we can be purified and come
forth as gold!"

Shadrach, Meshach, and Abednego had to either bow to
the Babylonian king's idolatrous image or be thrown into a
fiery furnace to be burned alive. To paraphrase them, "We do
not know if our God will deliver us from the fire, but we know
He is able! Anyway, we will not bow to worship your image!"
The three Hebrew children realized they would win either way.
If they died, they would be in the presence of their Lord for all
eternity. If they lived, they would experience an amazing
demonstration and testimony of God's omnipotence. Of
course, you know the story, God miraculously delivered them,
with not even the smell of smoke on their clothes!

Do not be quick to be influenced by those who pressure
us to conform to the world's methods and trends. Jesus will
show Himself mighty in our lives if we will remain faithful and
true to Him. The Hebrew children were not at all worried,
upset, nor did they complain about their dire circumstances,
and neither should we. We should be at peace, knowing the
Most High God has His hand upon us.

God usually does not deliver believers from the fire; He
delivers us through the fire! "When thou passest through the
waters, I will be with thee; and through the rivers, they shall
not overflow thee: when thou walkest through the fire, thou
shalt not be burned; neither shall the flame kindle upon thee"
(Isaiah 43:2). Any children of God who may be going through

a difficult life experience today, please know that God is with us, and He never fails. He is doing a great work in us and revealing His glory through our lives. Be assured, on the other side of the fire is freedom and countless blessings! Stand strong and see the salvation of the Lord and His promises fulfilled!

Mustard Seed Faith

And the Lord said, If you had faith as a grain of mustard seed, you could say unto this sycamine tree, Be plucked up by the root, and be planted in the sea; and it would obey you.

Luke 17:6

A mustard seed is considered the smallest of seeds on earth, yet it can grow into a very large tree. Jesus uses the mustard seed to illustrate how a small amount of faith in Him can result in miraculous and unimaginable outcomes. Genuine faith is powerful, even in small doses!

If we have mustard seed faith, we can realize miracles! Real faith can rid the world of a global pandemic, see America return to Christian principles, and cause our government leaders to seek God before making important decisions that affect our lives. "For by grace are you saved through faith" (Ephesians 2:8); and "Without faith, it is impossible to please God..." (Hebrews 11:6). If we truly believe, Jesus will do great and mighty things!

Whatever mountainous obstacle may be standing in our way today, we should allow faith to arise within and watch God move it out of the way to fulfill His purpose in us. Jesus wants us to restore and build upon our faith daily. Do you desire mustard seed faith? We began the faith process by reading, memorizing, and meditating on Scripture, for "faith comes by hearing, and hearing by the word of God" (Romans 10:17). With God, all things are possible!

Dare to Dream

...Write the vision, and make it plain upon tables, that he may run who reads it.

Habakkuk 2:2

Today's Scripture encourages us to write important things down. There is amazing power in writing down our goals, inspiration, and vision. When we write these down, we proactively and sometimes even subconsciously plan toward fulfilling them. By writing them down, we determine not to simply react to life, but to work toward achieving our dreams and goals.

God wants us to act on the dreams that He has given us. We take ownership of them by planning and preparing for them. Success is not accidental. We should write down clearly established goals for where we see ourselves in our careers, finances, and relationships with God and people. Then begin moving toward these goals in incremental stages. We cannot possibly know in advance of how everything will happen, yet by keeping the faith and remaining obedient and properly aligned to the Word, Jesus will work supernaturally behind the scenes on our behalf to direct all things for our ultimate good.

Let us move toward realizing the dreams God has given us by writing down some goals and dreams for life. Write down some short-term goals (less than 1 year out), mid-term goals (1-5 years out), and long term (more than 5 years out). Make sure the shorter-term goals build toward the long-term goals. Then, ask Jesus for His wisdom on how to accomplish our goals. Jesus will give us wisdom, insight, and favor as we take steps to bring our dreams to pass.

Returning to Our First Love

Remember his marvelous works that he has done; his wonders, and the judgments of his mouth.

Psalm 105:5

In the world of constant responsibilities with our careers and family obligations, we can easily fall into a routine where our life can seem mundane. Anything can become monotonous and mundane after some time if we let it.

Remember when we first gave our hearts to Jesus, the thrill and excitement of being a new convert. We were so full of joy and love that it simply blew our minds! It was truly joy, unspeakable and full of glory! Yet, we frequently fall into the routine of Christian life of doing what we are supposed to be doing without even thinking. Yet, the joy and excitement may have dissipated. Jesus wants to restore the thrill and love of serving Him again. We can do this by remembering His marvelous works, His wonders, and judgments!

We should be aware of the danger of leaving our first love for the Lord. Long ago, the church in Ephesus was busy doing many things for God, yet Jesus said, "I have somewhat against thee, because thou hast left thy first love" (Revelation 2:4). Our love for God should be foremost in our hearts. Jesus identified the greatest of all commandments: "Thou shalt love the Lord thy God with all thy heart, and with all thy soul, and with all thy mind, and with all thy strength: this is the first commandment" (Mark 12:30).

Let us return to our first love for the Lord! "Ye shall seek me, and find me, when ye shall search for me with all your heart. And I will be found of you . . ." (Jeremiah 29:13). If our love for God has grown cold, take steps to renew our relationship with Him, and return to our first love. He waits for us with open arms.

Our Healer

He heals the broken in heart, and binds up their wounds.

Psalm 147:3

Regardless of what may be broken in our lives, Jesus can bring us complete healing. He is the Great Physician and the Son of Righteousness rising with healing in His wings. He will heal our mind, body, soul, finances, relationships. Jesus is right for whatever is wrong in our lives!

Just as a doctor may wrap a broken arm in a cast, Jesus will surround us and wrap us in His loving presence. As we go through His healing process, He places Himself over our brokenness and protects our injured area until it has time to heal and become strong enough again to be used properly. Our God makes all things new! He restores our weary soul and makes us completely whole!

Even if we are currently going through the healing process, let us thank God for protecting and healing us. Jesus will restore us better and stronger than before! Release any brokenness to Him and let Him be our healer today

Complete Devotion

And you shall seek me, and find me, when you shall search for me with all your heart.

Jeremiah 29:13

Jesus wants us to seek Him, for we were made to seek him! However, we often are guilty of seeking God along with the other things that distract us for our devotion to Him. We never should allow anything to diminish the Lord from having priority and full devotion of our heart. Only Jesus is worthy of complete devotion!

Jesus has benefits and rewards already in place awaiting us, ready to be released to us. All we need to do to receive them is to seek Him and search for Him with all our heart! If we will arise early to spend time in His presence and in Scripture, thank Him for all His goodness, and make Him our first priority, His blessings will overtake us.

May Jesus bless us with an undivided heart, one that seeks Him as the number one priority. Ask Him to forgive us for letting other people and things distract our focus from Him and allowing them to interfere with our devotion and service to His Kingdom. May He fill us with a holy passion for His will above all other concerns and interests.

Today, there is nothing or no one more important than seeking Jesus in all our ways. As we go about our day, let us keep Him on our mind and in our heart. Seek Him and ask for His guidance. If we truly search for Him, we will find Him and the peace, blessing, joy, and power He provides every day of our life!

Set Trust and Obey

Now therefore, if ye will obey my voice indeed, and keep my covenant, then ye shall be a peculiar treasure unto me above all people: for all the earth is mine.

Exodus 19:5

If we are to achieve our greatest potential, we must trust and obey God. We should obey Him even if we do not understand why or if what He has asked us to do appears irrational. Genuine faith is trusting Jesus enough to do whatever He asks us to do!

Trust and obey even when it seems illogical. If we have everything we need and circumstances are already in place for us, this does not require faith. Sometimes Jesus will ask us to do things that seem strange and unpractical. However, each time we trust and obey, a blessing comes to us. He rewards obedience.

If we know that Jesus loves us, we should never question a command from Him. His command will always be what is right and best. Anytime He gives us a command, we are not to only observe or debate it. We are to obey it! We will not obey Him, if we do not believe and trust Him. We cannot believe Him if we do not love Him. We cannot love Him unless we know Him!

"Faith never knows where it is being led, but it loves and knows the one who is leading" (Oswald Chambers). Today, let us choose to let go of carnal reasoning and simply trust and obey God.

Arise and Shine

Arise, shine; for your light has come, and the glory of the Lord has risen upon you.

Isaiah 60:1

Regardless of what difficulties we are currently going through, God is telling us today to "Arise and shine!" If one door has closed, Jesus will open a new one for us. Our setback is a springboard for our comeback!

If our job is not working out the way we planned, do not be discouraged. Find another job. If friends have betrayed us and our hearts broken in relationships, do not sit around lonely and depressed. Make some new friends. Arise from the ashes of despair into the light, joy, and glory of the Lord!

The enemy tries to make us believe that we are not good enough, that God cannot use us, that things will never get better, and that we should just stop trying. Satan's goal is to keep us down. But Jesus wants us to ARISE! We do not need to have everything figured out. We just need to be willing to get up and try!

As we keep offering ourselves to Jesus, letting Him fill us with His love and His grace, He empowers us to live the way He wants us to live. We are not in this alone. Our God is always nearby. He is ready and willing to help. One key to bouncing back is by taking time to share God's love to the people around us. As we allow His light to shine into us and out to others more and more, we will be transformed. We begin to shine a little bit brighter every day.

Learning to Let Go

Remember you not the former things, neither consider the things of old.

Isaiah 43:18

The past is gone. It is finished. We cannot reclaim it, nor can we undo it. Today is a new day, a fresh opportunity, and the time to live our faith in Jesus. Let us press onward, trusting that our God will keep us and supply all we need for the journey forward.

Often, we miss out on living a victorious life, because we keep dwelling on past disappointments and mistakes. We begin to think that we have failed too many times to ever recover and to be of any benefit to anyone, especially Jesus. Our negative thinking can prevent us from our divine purpose. If we are to live victoriously, we must learn to release the past and to keep hope for our future.

May we learn from our mistakes, but not dwell on them. May we never rest on our previous accomplishments but use them to further God's work in and through us. Let us forgive those who have hurt us. Paul tells us to forget those things which are behind. Now that we have learned from our past, it is time to put it behind us and to "press toward the high calling of God!"

Destined to Bear Fruit

I am the vine, you are the branches: He who abides in me, and I in him, the same brings forth much fruit: for without me you can do nothing.

John 15:5

By remaining intimately attached to Jesus we take on His nature and character. We bear fruit of Him. As we obey His word, the very Spirit of Christ Jesus abides within, and He reveals Himself to us. We become like Him in thoughts and deeds. The gulf between Heaven and Earth lessens with each passing day, for Jesus dwells within. In Him we live and move and have our being.

The life of the tree branch depends on being connected to the vine. If it is not attached, it will die. If we attempt to live our lives separate from Jesus, we will die. We can do nothing without Him. For the life-giving and fruit-producing source of the True Vine to continue flowing to us, we must remain attached to Him. We stay connected by seeking Him daily in prayer, reading and meditating on Bible Scripture, and worshipping Him in spirit and in truth. Then, our life will bear fruits of joy, love, peace, patience, kindness, faith, meekness, and self-control.

If we abide in Him, we will bear "much fruit." More than simply getting by God's blessings will overflow and we will experience an abundant harvest. He wants to plentifully supply all our needs according to His riches in glory! Make Jesus first priority in our lives right now and we will be blessed in everything we do in life!

Time to Reboot

And be not conformed to this world: but be transformed by the renewing of your mind, that you may prove what is that good, and acceptable, and perfect, will of God.

Romans 12:2

Do not become conformed to the world nor influenced by it. This is extremely difficult to guard against. Today's verse reminds us that our mind is our greatest battlefield. Wrong thinking can be dangerous because we are constantly fed messages from various media and other worldly influences that try to distort God's truth and holy values in our lives. Rather than being approved by the world by acting like the world, we should be transformed by the renewing of our minds and by bringing every thought, word, and deed into obedience to Christ Jesus and His ways!

Our mind functions like a computer. The way we program the mind is how it will work. We could have the best and most expensive computer in the world, but if the software installed in it is corrupted, it will be contaminated and can never work properly until the computer virus is removed. Our "hardware" is fearfully and wonderfully made to work perfectly in this world. We were created to live life abundantly. God programmed us this way, to be the head and not the tail. The reason we do not always live the way we were designed to live is because we have allowed worldly influence to contaminate our "software"—i.e., our mind, will, and emotions. Today, we need to run the antivirus of God's Word through our entire system and reboot through prayer and worship. Only Jesus can restore us to our original pure working condition.

May Jesus guard our soul from pride, our heart from callousness, and our mind from too much emphasis on worldly pleasure and may He help us to remain focused on His will before anything else. May He teach us in our heart what it truly means to be about our Heavenly Father's business, especially in our thought-life!

Everlasting Father

For unto us a child is born, unto us a son is given: and the government shall be upon his shoulder: and his name shall be called Wonderful, Counsellor, The mighty God, The everlasting Father, The Prince of Peace.

Isaiah 9:6

Jesus Christ said, "When you see me, you see the Father." He is the Everlasting Father that Isaiah prophesied about over 600 years before His arrival as a babe in a manger. Oh, wonder of wonders, how could it be, that God became flesh and was given for me!

When we ask Jesus to become the Lord and Savior of our lives, we become children of the Most High God. We immediately have an Everlasting Father, who will never leave nor forsake us. He is the good and perfect Father who loves us with an everlasting love. Jesus loves us as we are, yet He patiently and lovingly guides us and builds His character within us helping us to become the best we can possibly be for His glory.

Let us praise our Everlasting Father today for loving us and for always being present on our behalf. May we experience His love deeper with each passing day, so we may know Him greater. May His love emit from us so others can realize His kindness and power and begin to know Jesus as their Everlasting Father too.

Accepted of God

…Of a truth I perceive that God is no respecter of persons: But in every nation he that fears him, and works righteousness, is accepted with him.

Acts 10:34-35

God provides the same opportunities to all, regardless of ethnicity, race, heritage, and gender. "Whosoever shall call on the name of the Lord shall be saved" (Acts 2:21). His desire is to bring freedom to everyone that will fear Him, choose righteousness, and live according to His Word. Jesus desires to liberate us from everything holding us back in life, so He can release His abundant blessings upon us.

Jesus looks upon our hearts and knows our motives. Nothing can be hidden from our omniscient God. He also sees the talents and potential He has put within us. Refuse to allow Satan and his emps to feed us lies, telling us that Jesus will bless everyone but us. Open our eyes and see the blessings He has already provided. He has many more in the pipeline coming our way!

Begin by thanking Jesus for great salvation, for His unfailing love, and for freedom in our soul! Focus on honoring Him and doing what is right. By doing this, we position ourselves to receive His favor and abundance. Choose to do what is right and honor Jesus with our attitude, words, and actions. May the Holy Spirit reveal to us any area of our life displeasing to Him. May we be living epistles of God and pure examples of a real Christian, which will cause others to desire a wonderful life in Jesus too!

United We Stand

Where there is neither Greek nor Jew, circumcision nor uncircumcision,
Barbarian, Scythian, bond nor free: but Christ is all, and in all...

Colossians 3:11

In the new life of a Christian, one's nationality or race or education or social position is unimportant; such things mean nothing. Whether a person has Jesus Christ is what matters, and He is equally available to all.

When Jesus looks at us, He does not see different color, race, social standing, or intellectual level. The world focuses on what we wear, what we drive and how we look. He sees beyond the superficial things that our society constantly magnifies. Jesus sees us through eyes of pure and undefiled love.

People often make hasty generalizations of whole groups of people based on the actions of a few. If we have been seeing people through the world's preconceived lens, let us open our eyes and hearts to seeing them as Jesus sees them. He has allowed us all to be in this place at this time in history by His masterful design, and He has a divine purpose for each of us. As we see through God's eyes, we join in unity, become stronger and more powerful against the real enemy of humanity, the ultimate deceiver Satan, who works tirelessly to keep us alienated from one another. For a people divided cannot stand. Christian people united are invincible, in the name of Jesus!

Today, let go of any prejudice. Ask Jesus to fill our hearts with His love and to help us to see others the way He see us all. Praise Him for the work He has done in our lives and for the many blessings and opportunities He has provided.

Holy Spirit Change Me!

But we all, with open face beholding as in a glass the glory of the Lord, are changed into the same image from glory to glory, even as by the Spirit of the Lord is good to the use of edifying, that it may minister grace unto the hearers.

II Corinthians 3:18

Our change to become more like Jesus is an ongoing process. The Holy Spirit continually works within, molding us into His image. We need to continue looking to Jesus, trusting His Spirit to make us more like Him each day.

Our lives reflect God's goodness. When we are joyful, patient, projecting confidence, show love toward others, and advancing in each area of our lives, we reflect His goodness. Remember, Jesus desires for us to prosper and be in health even as our soul prospers. As we walk in His will daily, God releases and pours out His blessing and favor upon us and we become a reflection of our Heavenly Father. He delights in us!

We should ask Jesus to forgive us for the times we have allowed our faith to become complacent and have lost our focus on Him. May He bless us as we attempt to be more intentional in our plans to become more like Him and to reach spiritual maturity. Praise Him for showing us His goodness and faithfulness. May we represent Jesus well in the midst of a dark world.

A Heart for God

A new heart also will I give you, and a new spirit will I put within you: and I will take away the stony heart out of your flesh, and I will give you a heart of flesh.

Ezekiel 36:26

When Jesus enters our soul, He gives us a spiritual heart transplant. The Lord gives us a new heart! God does this because our old heart of sin is spiritually as hard as a rock and could not receive or understand the things of God. A heart filled with sin cannot obey God or even yearn for the things of God.

When we accept Christ Jesus in our life as our Lord and Savior, not only does He give us a new heart, our bloodline changes. We become children of the King of kings and the Lord of lords! We become subject to a heavenly birthright! God's spiritual favor supersedes any curse in the carnal realm. When we truly realize who we are in Jesus, we cannot become bitter about the temporary circumstances of this life, for we know that nothing can prevent us from achieving our divine destiny!

After Jesus gives us a new heart and a new life, we desire to please Him rather than ourselves. We desire to hear from Him so that we can know how to please Him and what we must do to obey Him. We acquire a hunger for His Word because we understand it contains His instructions for our lives and confirms His voice to us. We desire to be with Jesus, so we seize opportunities to have fellowship with Him in prayer and worship. When we follow Jesus, we are choosing our godly heritage of abundant and eternal life.

May we live for Him and follow Him wherever He may lead us. May our insatiable longing for Jesus grow more intense in our hearts daily. We do not desire to do the things we used to do because we only desire to please Him. With our new heart, we have become people after God's own heart!

Lord, Change Me

Therefore if any man be in Christ, he is a new creature: old things are passed away; behold, all things have become new.

II Corinthians 5:17

To move forward with our lives in a positive way, we must let go of our past. We all have things that have happened to us or things that we have done that we are not proud of. Holding on to the past prevents us from pressing forward in God's plan for our lives. When we turn to Jesus Christ with all our heart, we immediately have a fresh start, a clean slate, and a new beginning! Hallelujah!

Whenever our past tries to haunt us and people try to recall the sins of our past, remember that our all-knowing Creator has cast all our sins into the depths of the sea, never to be remembered again by Him. To begin our new life in Jesus, we must trust what He says about us, rather than what people think and speak. Scripture says we are pure and holy children of God.

Something else we must do to prevent our past from controlling our present and future is to commit our lives completely to Jesus Christ. Make Him our number one priority in every decision and in all we say and do. We must move beyond our past before we can step into God's calling for our lives.

When we become free from our past, we will begin to make a positive impact on the lives of others, helping them to find new life in God and hope for their future too. If thoughts of failure and disappointment have filled our minds lately, through prayer we can allow Jesus to transform our minds into positive thoughts of freedom and redemption. If we want to see our world change for the better, let us start by praying,

"Jesus please change me, mold me, and shape me into your image!"

Clean Hands and a Pure Heart

Who shall ascend into the hill of the Lord? or who shall stand in his holy place? He who has clean hands, and a pure heart; who has not lifted up his soul unto vanity, nor sworn deceitfully. He shall receive the blessing from the Lord, and righteousness from the God of his salvation.

Psalm 24:3-5

Jesus desires that we receive every blessing that He has in store for us. Today's passage informs us about how we can obtain His wonderful blessings, by having clean hands and a pure heart!

The blood of Jesus cleanses us from all sin when we truly repent and surrender our hearts to Him, allowing Him to become Savior and Lord of our lives. However, the enemy is constantly trying to cause us to have impure hearts. We can allow him a small opening by exposing ourselves to false philosophy or perversion on TV or the Internet. As we surrender territory to the enemy, sin becomes a bad habit which robs us of our time and pollutes our minds, eating away at our soul.

We should determine to liberate ourselves by turning away from anything displeasing to the Lord and that could be an obstacle to obtaining God's favor and blessings. Choose to be a person of integrity and of excellence. May we resolve to live a life pleasing unto Jesus, so we can "ascend unto the hill of the Lord and stand in His holy place!"

Jumpstart Faith

And all things, whatsoever you shall ask in prayer, believing, you shall
receive.

Matthew 21:22

Scripture declares numerous promises from God to His people. He has blessed us with all spiritual blessings. He has made us worthy and more than conquerors. Jesus promises to always be near and to never forsake us. His mercy and compassion are fresh and everlasting toward us. These promises are already settled and done because of what Jesus did for us on calvary's cross. His death, burial, and resurrection sealed all these scriptural promises for us, and no one can take them away! To access them, we simply need to start believing.

To jumpstart our faith in God's promises, we should praise and thank Him for every promised blessing He provides. Eye has not seen, nor ear heard all that God has in store for those who love Him. In our minds, we can only imagine all that awaits us. He wants to do exceedingly above all we could ask or think! Thank and praise Him for His bountifully supply of whatever we need and for all His goodness toward us! When we lift our hearts and voices in praise and adoration to Jesus Christ, we prepare ourselves to receive even more from Him, for Jesus loves the praises of His people. If there was ever a secret to unleashing His power, favor, and blessings in any situation, it is developing a heart of true thanksgiving and praise!

Rivers in the Desert

Behold, I will do a new thing; now it shall spring forth; shall you not know it? I will even make a way in the wilderness, and rivers in the desert.

Isaiah 43:19

Today's verse was written during a time when the Israelites suffered under Babylonian exile. Isaiah had reminded them of all God had done for them in the past, particularly of how He miraculously delivered them from Egyptian bondage. Isaiah informed them not to become stuck in the past, but to look forward in faith of the new thing God would do for them.

Jesus desires to do something brand new in our lives. Regardless of the struggles or the dry and barren season we may currently be experiencing, our God will make a way in the wilderness and rivers in the desert! Hallelujah! In the place of what can seem like total desolation to us, Jesus will liberate us and shower us with overflowing power and anointing.

Amid impossibility is where God makes His promise. We may feel forsaken and forgotten, yet Jesus has a promise for us. He will do something new and amazing! We had to first endure the wilderness to arrive at it. The wasteland was necessary for us to see Him perform His greatest work! He allowed us to go through the dry place on our way to possessing His promise. Our steps have been divinely ordered by Jesus.

The desert is the catalyst for our destiny! When we are down to nothing, Jesus is up to something. Praise God today for we are coming out of the dry and barren land to rivers of living water, in the name of Jesus!

Name Above All Names

Wherefore God also has highly exalted him, and given him a name which is above every name: That at the name of Jesus every knee should bow, of things in heaven, and things in earth, and things under the earth.

Philippians 2:9

The name of Jesus is above every name in Heaven and on Earth. His name is greater and more eminent than every other name that is named, for His name is the most excellent name that is named in heaven or earth, throughout time and into eternity.

His name is greater than earthly kings, presidents, or individuals of great wealth and prestige. His name is far above and more powerful than Kennedy, Rockefeller, Bezos, Trump, Gates, Zuckerberg, and Buffet. The name of Jesus supersedes any other known name. His name has power over all sin, sickness, poverty, and authority. Only the name of Jesus provides salvation, healing, power, love, joy, peace, deliverance, provision, and blessings. The list of all that is available to us through His name is limitless.

God says, "…I have even called you by your name: I have surnamed you…" (Isaiah 45:4). By taking on His name, we have been granted God's power and authority, having access to His storehouse of blessings. Everything He has is available to us in the name of Jesus. "If you shall ask anything in my name, I will do it" (John 14:14).

Jesus alone is to be highly exalted. He alone is to be worshipped and honored. He alone is God Almighty, the Lord of heaven and earth forever and ever!

Go Forth with Joy

For ye shall go out with joy and be led forth with peace…

Isaiah 55:12

Being full of joy is evidence that we are full of God, for the joy of the Lord is our strength and in His presence is fullness of joy. We should arise each morning with eagerness and feeling thrilled about the future awaiting us.

Since every day is a gift from God, we should have a spring in our step and a smile on our face as we follow our life's dreams with passion. If we go out with joy, Jesus will guide us into the very place we need to be, help us to make the right decisions, and have a peace about everything. When we are full of joy, we have God's favor. When we have His favor, new opportunities avail themselves to us and we can expect spiritual promotion, as well as promotion in the natural.

Jesus did not save us for us to sit around and complain about all our problems and to merely try to get through the day. We are created in His image, crowned with His righteousness and glory, and empowered by the Holy Spirit. Regardless of any recent setbacks we may have experienced, today is a new day! Jesus desires to restore to us the joy of salvation and of living.

May the fire and passion of the Holy Spirit be rekindled to burn bright within us and in all we do. Let us begin by praising God for another wonderful day, filled with fresh opportunities in serving and loving Him. When our lives are filled with peace, faith and joy, others will want what we have. May we remain full of joy, so we may serve Jesus with our whole heart.

Believe and Speak Boldly

We, having the same spirit of faith, according as it is written, I believed, and therefore have I spoken; we also believe, and therefore speak.

II Corinthians 4:13

We boldly say what we believe, trusting God to care for us, just as the psalmist of the Old Testament did when he said, "I believe and therefore I speak." Where there is true faith, and the true Spirit of faith, we will speak of, for, and in the name of Jesus Christ, as we should: for as "with the heart man believeth unto righteousness, so with the mouth confession is made unto salvation" (Romans 10:10). We boldly declare His great name, sincerely and faithfully without the fear of men.

When we truly believe God, we declare His wonderful promises and mighty works in faith. We speak words of faith over nonexistent things as though they are. By doing this, we position ourselves for a miracle. We place ourselves under the windows of heaven by obeying His commandments. By declaring His Word, we open the door for Him to move mightily on our behalf. Remain faithful, keep standing, continue believing, and keep speaking, and we will receive the glorious victory and blessings Jesus has awaiting us!

Praise the Lord Jesus for His Word, which is Spirit and Life! Let us set our minds and hearts on Him and declare His promises. Give Him thanksgiving and honor for His faithfulness toward us, as we press onward in His plan for us. "So that we may boldly say, The Lord is my helper, and I will not fear what man shall do unto me" (Hebrews 13:6).

All We Need Is Jesus

And God said unto Moses, I Am Who I Am: and he said, Thus shalt thou say unto the children of Israel, I Am has sent me unto you.

Exodus 3:14

Jesus is the great and mighty God! He is the Creator of the universe, the One who spoke the world into existence (see John 1:3). He is the I Am, Yahweh, Jehovah, of the Old Testament, who spoke at the burning bush unto Moses. When He came to Earth as a man in the New Testament, He revealed who He truly is by saying, "I am the way, the truth, and the life…I am the resurrection and the life…Before Abraham was, I am!"

The verse signifies the real being of God, His self-existence, and that He is the Being of beings. It reveals His eternity and immutability, dependability, and faithfulness in fulfilling His promises, for this includes all time, past, present, and future. He is the Great I AM declaring to each of us today, "I am all you need. I am your strength, shepherd, provider, healer, righteousness, sanctifier, peace, problem solver, way maker, and your victory!"

Rather than focusing on how big our problems are today, we should focus on how great and mighty Jesus is! He is everything we need! His power is not limited by our circumstance. Faith is a catalyst that helps us experience the manifestation of God's power in our lives. Jesus is the Great I AM!

Thank God for Letting It Happen

In everything give thanks: for this is the will of God in Christ Jesus concerning you.

I Thessalonians 5:18

Thank God for letting it happen! The Bible is filled with accounts of pain, rejection, and turmoil in which God turned hardship and heartache into a blessing for His children. Jonah found himself in what he described as the "belly of hell," yet after the experience, the Word of the Lord came unto him the second time. The ultimate betrayal of Joseph's brothers was the catalyst to his becoming a powerful and influential leader in Egypt, positioned to rescue his family from imminent starvation. Paul spent most of his years of ministry as a prisoner for the gospel. While in prison, he wrote half of the New Testament books. He said, "Wherein I suffer trouble, as an evil doer, even unto bonds; but the word of God is not bound" (II Timothy 2:9). We will never experience the fullness of what God wants us to gain from life's painful experiences until we are able to thank Him for letting it happen!

Regardless of what we may have gone through in our past, whether it be abuse, betrayal, loss, sickness, or pain, Jesus desires to turn it all into a blessing for us. It is time to stop allowing our past experiences to defeat us. Now is the time to move forward to the hope and opportunities Jesus has in store. Pain and suffering should cause us to run to a deeper and more intimate place in Christ Jesus, rather than into a depressed state of hopelessness.

Jesus wants to turn our suffering into victory and our sorrow into laughter. As children of God, we can rest assured that, whatever has happened in our lives, He intends to use it for our good. "And we know that all things work together for good to them that love God…" (Romans 8:28). If Jesus had not suffered and died on the cross in agony, we would not have access to His cleansing blood or know Him as our Savior and Lord. Because He died and rose again, we have abundant life and hope of a glorious heavenly home awaiting us, where there will be no more sorrow, crying, or pain. Thank God for letting it happen!

The Journey to Permanent Provision

But my God shall supply all your need according to his riches in glory by Christ Jesus.

Philippians 4:19

Jesus promises to supply all our need. The key is for us to trust Him to satisfy what we most need in Him. When our hearts long to be full of Him, to be pleasing to Him, and to be blessed by His presence, we can confidently rely on Jesus supplying all we really need!

When the Israelites were in the desert, traveling to the Promised Land, God gave them manna to eat. The manna sustained them for a period, yet it was not permanent provision. Then, the manna stopped. Consequently, they had to move forward, and subsequently God gave them quail to eat. Quail nourished them for a time, but it was also momentary. God provided the children of Israel provisionally on their journey to the Promised Land, where permanent provision was in store for them. Knowing that the Lord had much greater ahead for them is what kept them moving forward on their journey. He could have kept them with manna or quail the entire time, but He wanted them to have better.

Jesus always has better in store for us if we will just keep moving forward. We should not allow ourselves to become too comfortable and think this is going to always last. Instead, we should be ready to adjust and be prepared to try new ways of doing things. If our "manna" or "quail" stops coming, do not become troubled. Keep moving forward and be prepared for the new provision Jesus has in store for us!

May Jesus open our eyes to see all the many wonderful ways He is providing for us and graciously providing the abundance He has poured into our lives. Do not allow our vision to be shortsighted and narrow. He has blessed us with much more than we can even see and greater is always in store. Thank Him for always providing for us and for leading and guiding us to better days and greater supply.

Words Matter

Death and life are in the power of the tongue: and they that love it shall eat the fruit thereof.

Proverbs 18:21

Words do matter. Irrespective of whether we think, speak, read, or write words, they can be used for good or bad, for positivity or negativity, to build up or to tear down, and to promote unity or division. Words have power to do the greatest good and the worst evil. We will be held accountable for every idle word we speak. Every careless word may come back to haunt us. Words are extremely powerful; take them seriously. Words can be our redemption, yet words can also be our downfall.

We can choose to use the force of our words constructively or destructively. Words have the ability to help, heal, hinder, hurt, harm, humiliate and humble. They leave a lasting impact long after they were used, even though we may forget having said them. The result of words lingers, good or bad, on those affected by them. Words are like seeds that land in our hearts instead of on the ground. Be careful what we plant and what we say. We may have to eat what we have planted someday.

The phrase "Sticks and stones may break my bones, but words will never hurt me," is completely false. Words can be forgiven, but not soon forgotten. We should be mindful when it comes to our words, though they may not mean a great deal to us, they can remain with others for a lifetime. The wrong words cause pain; the right words cause hope. A life can be changed forever with uplifting words. "A word fitly spoken is like apples of gold in pictures of silver" (Proverbs 25:11). One kind word can change someone's entire day. Speak words today that are kind, loving, positive, uplifting, encouraging, and life-giving.

Light of the World

Then spoke Jesus again unto them, saying, I am the light of the world: he who follows me shall not walk in darkness, but shall have the light of life.

John 8:12

Jesus is the light within our world. "This little light of mine, I'm gonna let it shine…Won't let Satan blow it out. I'm gonna let it shine…Hide it under a bushel? No! I'm gonna let it shine…Let it shine til Jesus comes. I'm gonna let it shine." Today is the day to shine bright for Jesus!

Darkness is more than a figure in this verse. It is a pervasive way of living and viewing the world. Darkness is where deception, evil, crime, predators, sin, and death abide. Following Jesus means to have Him in our heart and allowing Him to cast away the darkness that afflicts us internally, so we will not fear darkness on the outside. Jesus gives light, yet His light does more than just permeate light in a dark room. His light illuminates our heart.

Jesus, the Light of the World, declares that now we are the light of the world. He expects His light to be reflected brightly through us daily for all the world to see and to hopefully draw others to Him. So many are groping around lost in the darkness, but we can shine the way to salvation. We do not sit around in the darkness in our homes at night. We switch the light on powered by electricity. It is high time for us to turn on the light of Jesus's love and truth, powered by the Holy Spirit, so we may shine brightly too!

Jesus said, "Anyone who follows Me will never walk in the darkness but will have the light of life." Lights are meant to be seen. They are meant to guide our way when it is dark. And the light of Christ is meant to shine through us so that those looking for Him can find Him. Consider how we can let our light shine today for Jesus. Let us begin by praising Him for casting away the dark fears of our lives that so easily envelop us and pray for strength and courage to not only live in the light, but to also guide others to the light.

Prepare for Greater

Enlarge the place of your tent, and let them stretch forth the curtains of your habitations: spare not, lengthen your cords, and strengthen your stakes.

Isaiah 54:2

Prepare ourselves for the increase. Our future with God is bright and promising! God desires to abundantly bless His people. As we align ourselves with scriptural principles, the Lord will open the windows of Heaven and pour out unimaginable blessings.

We need to expand our capacity to receive. If we have only a bushel size basket, and someone wants to give us a hundred bushels of supplies, the problem is with our limited capacity, not with the supply. We need a bigger basket! In the same manner, Jesus wants us to expand our vision to make room for the overabundance of new favor and blessing He wants to provide us with.

The earth is the Lord's, and the fulness thereof; the world, and they that dwell therein" (Psalm 24:1). The key to receiving greater blessing is to first be thankful for what we have. Secondly, we truly have faith to believe that it is His will to prosper us. Finally, we confidently anticipate and prepare ourselves to receive all He desires for us. Despite how many blessings we expect from God, He continually exceeds our expectations! "God has a way of giving by the cartloads to those who give away by shovelfuls" (Charles Spurgeon). Our God daily loads us with benefits! May we release our limited thinking and old mindsets. Let us open ourselves to everything Jesus has in store.

Anticipating the Unimaginable

But as it is written, Eye hath not seen, nor ear heard, neither have entered into the heart of man, the things which God has prepared for them who love him.

I Corinthians 2:9

We dream and anticipate about many things which are less glorious in real life than they were in our imaginations. However, one impending event will be much greater than we could ever imagine, the return of Jesus Christ to take His waiting bride, His church, to our heavenly home! Even so, come quickly Lord Jesus!

Today's verse also encourages us to increase our expectancy level. We think we are blessed now, yet we have not seen anything yet! He has wonderful things in store for our future. If He told us, it would blow our minds! Jesus wants us to bless our future and everything we put our hand to do. He desires to shower us with His favor, goodness, and blessings which are unfathomable to us! Impossibilities with men are opportunities to God!

Prepare for increase and for greater. Remove all limits from our minds. Jesus can do exceedingly, abundantly above all we can ask or imagine. Keep on believing, keep obeying His Word, and keep our hearts open to the impossible, for with God all things are possible! We have not seen anything yet!

Trust What Jesus Says

*And the angel of the Lord appeared unto him, and said unto him, The
Lord is with you, mighty man of valor.*

Judges 6:12

Gideon was going through a period in his life when his
faith was weak. At this moment of discouragement, an
angel appears to Gideon with a message from God to tell him
that the Lord is with him. God referred to Gideon as a "mighty
man of valor." However, Gideon doubted whether God really
meant this for him. Gideon was poor and the lowest degree in
his father's house. He perceived himself as weak and incapable,
but God perceived him as strong and confident!

Like Gideon, we have all experienced times in our life
when our faith was weak. Maybe we questioned if we really
heard from the Lord about something. Perhaps we felt as
though so much was against us in life that we could not go on.
The question is, will we believe what God says about us, or will
we believe what we feel and think and allow our circumstances
to dictate our attitude about life and our future. We may feel
weak, but Jesus says we are strong. We may feel like a victim,
but He says we are victorious. We may fear, but He says we are
courageous. We may be indebted, but He says we are
prosperous. We may be sick, yet He says we are healed. We
may be captivated to a sinful addiction; Jesus says we are free
indeed! We may feel incapable, yet He says we are able!

Just like Gideon, God will not leave us. He sees us in our
discouragement and tells us again and again in Scripture that
we can make it. Today, let us shift our mindset onto what His
Word says. Get into agreement with Him. In the face of our
circumstances, let us determine to trust what He says about us.
Jesus is for us, and He is with us every step of the way!

Peaceful Journey to the Promise Land

And Moses said unto the people, Fear not, stand still, and see the salvation of the Lord, which he will show to you today...The Lord shall fight for you, and you shall hold your peace.

Exodus 14:13-14

The Israelites had just been delivered from slavery and were journeying toward the Promise Land. They were ecstatic to finally be free! Pharaoh, however, had changed his mind about releasing them and had turned to pursing after them. As they arrived at the Red Sea, there seemed no way to escape. The situation seemed more than bleak. It looked impossible! They became fearful and began to complain, questioning why Moses had led them out of Egypt only to let them die. Moses replied, "Stand still and see the salvation of the Lord...The Lord will fight for you if you hold your peace and stop complaining." God showed Himself strong and once again delivered them!

For God to fight for and to liberate us, we too must get away from a negative mindset. Knowing Jesus will fight our battle means we do not have to distress or be discouraged when bad things happen in our lives. At those times when it seems the situation is hopeless or the circumstances at hand are too overwhelming, we may be tempted to doubt the Lord. We must remember that no problem is beyond the scope of His sovereign love and care for us.

Even if we are in the worst storm of our lives, do not allow it to steal our faith; simply trust in Jesus our Lord. Start recalling the countless times the Lord has fought our battles and delivered us in the past. He delivered us before and He will not fail us this time! Rest calmly and be at peace today, for Jesus will deliver us and He will lead us victoriously to the land of promise!

Greater than Ever!

The glory of this latter house shall be greater than of the former, saith the Lord of hosts: and in this place will I give peace...

Haggai 2:9

God promised that the 'final glory of His house' would eclipse its former glory, which must have seemed impossible to those lamenting elders. The final fulfilment of this magnificent prophecy is still future. Lasting peace will only happen when the Prince of Peace returns in the clouds of glory and sets His feet on the Mount of Olives, to bring in His Millennial Kingdom of peace and prosperity.

We the Church, are God's spiritual temple whom the Lord is using to fulfill His divine plans on Earth (see I Corinthians 6:19). The Holy Spirit indwells our mortal bodies. We have this treasure in clay vessels, so that the exceeding greatness of the power may be of God and not from ourselves. We live in a time of the Lord's increasing favor. He desires to do exceedingly abundantly above all we can imagine. We haven't seen anything yet! Jesus has favor in our future that will surpass all that we have seen previously.

Let hope rise within us today! Enlarge our vision. Confidently expect Jesus to bring fresh opportunities and blessings our way. Prepare our heart and mind to receive the increase He has for our future. The glory of this latter house shall be greater than the former! Praise God!

Nothing Can Stop Us

*What shall we then say to these things? If God be for us, who can be
against us?*

Romans 8:31

Paul asks a rhetorical question: "If God is for us, who can
be against us?" The unequivocal answer can only be "no
one!"

No matter what family curses from the past have tried to
dictate our future, they have no control over our destiny as
children of the Most High God. Jesus put His blessing and
favor on us, therefore no one can put a curse on us. Despite
the situations life throws at us, what circumstances beset us on
life's journey, or what difficulties we may face, our Lord in His
love and mercy, gathers up each and every experience, and uses
it for our eternal benefit and His greater glory. "Let us
therefore come boldly unto the throne of grace, that we may
obtain mercy, and find grace to help in time of need" (Hebrews
4:16).

God's intent is to redeem and bless, not to hurt. His
commitment is to work things out for our ultimate good, as He
is transforming us to be more like Him. Know that Jesus is for
us! Seek Him with a humble heart and break free from the
bondages of the past. Allow truth to define us and lead us to
victory, in Jesus name! When we choose to put Him first in our
life, nothing can stop His plan for us!

Resetting the Mind

And be not conformed to this world: but be transformed by the renewing of your mind, that you may prove what is that good, and acceptable, and perfect, will of God.

Romans 12:2

Do not be shaped by the world. This instruction can be very difficult to obey. It reminds us that our mind is the major battlefield where we fight. We daily battle messages constantly fed to us that twist God's Truth and godly values. Rather than being frustrated and influenced by the world or becoming like the world, we should be transformed by the renewing of our minds. We will then clearly recognize God's perfect will.

Many of us have grown up in an extremely poor environment, having no money, with limited educational and career opportunities. We may have been socially constructed amid poverty, mediocrity, or habitual sins. Yet, the Lord does not want us to succumb to that place. When we give our life to Jesus Christ, our mind and our thinking will be completely transformed from a defeated attitude to one of endless possibilities. With God, anything is possible! Seeds of greatness dwell inside each of us, ready to spring forth! We may be down, yet we are not out! We are children of the Most High God!

Regardless of what has occurred in our past, know that ultimately, we can reset our life for excellence and greatness. Release any wrong thoughts and worldly ideas and renew our minds according to Scipture. Let God's Truth saturate our heart and soul, so we can realize the greatness Jesus has in store!

Ordained of God for This Time

Before I formed you in the belly I knew you; and before you came forth out of the womb I sanctified you...

Jesus knows us with a special love and affection joined with it, in which sense the Lord knows us as His, not only before our formation in the womb, but before the foundation of the world! God loves us and has a wonderful plan for our life. This preparation began long before we were even conceived. He started getting us ready and the world ready for us, long before we were born.

God never made another one like anyone of us. He never made anyone else who can fill the place we can fill and do the things we can do. Each of us is unique, prepared of God for our time in history. Jesus has prepared us for this very hour and for this generation. What a gift we have! We are equipped for this moment, through the generations which lie behind us, that we might live, speak, and act in this time and for God's divine calling in our lives.

Jesus has a purpose for our life. No one can stop us from becoming all that God intended for us to be. We have been handpicked by Almighty God for this time and place! We should find confidence in His love, knowing that we are individuals of destiny and we are part of His mighty plan.

Let us thank Jesus for choosing us before we were ever born. Praise Him for knowing us and revealing Himself to us. Trust that He is working in our life daily, even when we do not perceive it. Stand in faith realizing that He has a wonderful plan for us!

TRUSTING THROUGH THE DARKNESS 103

Live Life with No Regrets

For do I now persuade men, or God? or do I seek to please men? for if I
yet pleased men, I should not be the servant of Christ.

Galatians 1:10

Paul was viciously attacked by fake Christians for his unwavering stand on the gospel truths. How much more do we, in these closing days of Christendom, need to be equally vigilant in our defense of the glorious gospel of Jesus?

Early on, Paul was passionate for the religious traditions of his family. However, after an encounter with Jesus, Paul discovered there was much more to his faith than what his family had taught him. Seeking his family and society's approval by following their traditions would have never provided Paul true salvation or a genuine relationship with God. Only faith in Jesus could change Paul's fate.

Every day we face the hard choice about where to put our trust. In those moments, we have to stop and ask the same question Paul did, "Am I trying to please God or men?" Serving Jesus, even though it goes contrary to the traditions of our friends and family, can be challenging. We should know that numerous individuals from their deathbeds have been asked, "What is your greatest regret?" Many have responded in a similar vein to this statement, "I wish I had not tried to please people and meet their expectations; and, I wish I had done more to please God and follow His plan for my life."

How many people today are not being true to who God created them to be simply because they are afraid they will disappoint someone or not be accepted? We cannot live trying to be who our family, coworkers, or friends want us to be. We must stay true to Jesus and what He has called us to be. Today, make the decision to live life with no regrets!

Daily Mercy and Compassion

It is of the Lord's mercies that we are not consumed, because his compassions fail not. They are new every morning: great is thy faithfulness

Lamentations 3:22-23

What keeps us through the night and gets us through the day, and will help us accomplish and even flourish in the coming days, are the mercies of Jesus. His mercy never fails nor ever ends! Every day brings a new supply of mercy to us. Jesus is faithful to ensure we have our daily need of it each morning. Praise be to the Lord for daily making us new and clean!

Have we done anything in our past that we are not proud of? Do we have decisions we regret? The wonderful news is that we do not have to live with the burden of guilt, shame, or condemnation from it any longer. God's mercies and compassion are flowing to us right now to liberate the heart mind, and soul, giving us a fresh start, a new beginning in Jesus name!

If there is anything haunting us from our past, appeal to the mercy of Jesus right now. Determine to release every weight from it. Call on His mercy and compassion, ask for forgiveness, and He will cleanse and refresh us now. Receive His love. Thank Him for the work He is doing in our life and bask in our new beginning.

Bridge Building through Confession

Confess your faults one to another, and pray one for another, that you may be healed. The effectual fervent prayer of a righteous man avails much.

James 5:16

Confessing our sins means we recognize sin for what it is in God's eyes and we are honest with Him and another trusted Christian about our flaws, failures, and sins. Confession not only results in forgiveness. It also leads to healing.

Honesty, humility, and openness should be the traits of every child of God. These characteristics are required for the shared support and disclosure among believers. The Lord expects us to be accountable to each other, to confess our sins as needed. Today's verse does not imply confessing our sins to a priest for absolution. It emphasizes accountability among believers. The point of this is to promote true confession and openness among ourselves and between us and God. Genuine confession prompts true repentance of sins committed. Honesty, humility, and accountability enable us to preserve fellowship with one another and with Jesus our Lord. Following this principle removes hindrances to our relationship with Jesus and the work of the Spirit in our lives.

Unconfessed sin negatively affects our prayer life as well as our walk with Jesus and the work He has called us to. Unconfessed sin causes separation between us and the Lord. Jesus will receive and honor our prayers when we communicate with Him honestly, in humility, and integrity. When we confess our sins, a spiritual bridge forms between us and God. Let us rebuild that bridge and maintain it daily through confession and accountability!

Obedient Faith

And when he saw them, he said unto them, Go show yourselves unto the priests. And it came to pass, that, as they went, they were cleansed.

Luke 17:14

Jesus told the lepers to go and show themselves to the priests, yet He did not heal them before they left from Him. He could have healed them right there but chose to wait for them to express their faith through obedience. After they went, as He had instructed them, they were healed. Healing occurred after they stepped out in faith and obeyed.

Far too often, many of God's children refuse to follow Him until He does what they want. We call Jesus our Lord and Master; however, we expect Him to provide our wants rather than yielding to Him as Lord of our life. If He truly is our Lord and Master, we will obey Him regardless of when we receive answers to our prayers. We should trust and obey Him, having faith in our loving and merciful Heavenly Father that He will work in our life the way that will most bless us for eternity.

Even if we do not receive our answer from Jesus right away, keep walking in His will. At times we may feel like giving up by saying, "What's the use?" Jesus is saying to us today, "If you do what I ask of you, you will be made whole." He wants us to put faith in action, even when it seems irrational or nonsensical. Let us keep moving forward in faith!

Open our eyes so we can see where and how we need to obey and follow. May Jesus grant us the patience that comes from the presence of His Holy Spirit. May His Spirit guide us to obedience, whether we see the answers right away or not. Surrender completely to Jesus, accepting Him truly as our Lord and Master.

Wonderfully Created

I will praise you; for I am fearfully and wonderfully made: marvelous are your works; and that my soul knows right well.

Psalm 139:14

We are made by our Heavenly Father! He even knew us before anyone knew we would exist. He planned our life before anyone planned our arrival. Our God has fearfully and wonderfully made us!

We all face difficulties and challenges, yet we possess hopes and dreams which may appear too incredible to comprehend. We face the decision to complain about our situation or we can determine to magnify and praise Jesus in the midst of it all; because, we have faith that He will eventually turn everything in our favor.

We must stop thinking and speaking negatively, for this inhibits the Lord from intervening on our behalf. Even when we do not envision our victory nor feel victorious, offer to Him sacrifices of praise anyhow! Jesus will then turn what seems like a curse into a blessing.

Jesus is great and greatly to be praised! Let us thank our Most High God, our Savior and Redeemer, for knowing us before we were ever able to know anything. Praise Him for choosing life for us. Honor Him with the gifts, abilities, and talents that He has given. May we live especially for Him for we are special to Him!

The Wellspring of Life

*But whosoever drinks of the water that I shall give him shall never thirst;
but the water that I shall give him shall be in him a well of water
springing up into everlasting life.*

John 4:14

Jesus is the only source of living water. In the midst of moral decay, violence, and disease, if there is anything this world needs, it is the hope that Jesus gives. Water is the precious gift for the tired and thirsty, the vital drink we all need. The water our Lord offers needs no purification. He promises a well of living water springing up unto eternal life!

When we become born again in Christ Jesus we transform into a new creature, made completely new internally. God puts within us an eternal well that never runs dry. We have an unlimited supply of good things inside which always bubbles to the outside. "The love of God is shed abroad in our hearts by the Holy Ghost which is given unto us!" (Romans 5:5). We have joy unspeakable and full of glory! The well of the Spirit flows endlessly springing up to produce wonderful fruits of love, joy, and peace in all we do and speak.

Thank God for the spring of eternal life and joy that He has placed within. Ask Him to help us to unclog any hindrances that may be blocking the free flow of kindness, peace, love, and laughter. May our life continuously display the joy and confidence that His refreshing presence brings.

Sweet Incense to God

For we are unto God a sweet savour of Christ, in them that are saved, and in them that perish.

2 Corinthians 2:15

Christian believers are to be a sweet fragrance to Jesus. Consider how pleasing the wonderful aroma of blossoming flowers are in springtime. Devoted Christians give off a delightful scent to God. This refers to the child of God who is growing in grace, firm in the faith, abiding in His will, and committed to being led by His Spirit. Our ministry and purpose is to show forth the fragrance of His love, not only with our lips but in our lives.

As we live our lives to please Jesus Christ, a beautiful fragrance captures His attention! The aroma of joy, peace, and love flowing from our lives is a sign that He is alive in us, and gives off an enjoyable incense to our Heavenly Father. Anytime we experience a pleasing smell, this should remind us that our consecrated life pleases Jesus.

May the incense of our life and prayers arise daily as a sweet fragrance to Jesus. Praise Him for always leading us to become more like Him. May we be comforted in realizing that the Most High God is pleased with our heart seeking after Him. As we continue to seek after Him, may we be that sweet-smelling savour and experience His glorious favor and blessing in every area of our life.

Sow Good Seed

He put forth another parable unto them, saying, The kingdom of heaven is likened unto a man which sowed good seed in his field: But while men slept, his enemy came and sowed tares among the wheat, and went his way.

Matthew 13:24-15

G God's work, disciples, and kingdom exist in a world which is under constant attack from the enemy. Satan's mission is to corrupt, pervert, and destabilize the Lord's work. The enemy wants to render the life message of Christians ineffective. Sometimes he conceals his tactics. Other times he attacks blatantly, seeking whom he may devour (see I Peter 5:8). We must be prepared for this spiritual warfare daily.

After we have planted good seed and weeds show up instead, which were planted by the enemy, we need to keep the right attitude and remain focused on the goodness of Jesus. Anytime these unexpected problems arise, we can take solace in knowing we did not cause them and expect with certainty that the Lord will intervene on our behalf.

Refuse to allow weeds to take root and keep all discouragement at bay. Let us look unto Jesus with eyes of faith. Continue praying, believing, and trusting for our harvest time is near. Jesus will show His power and deliver us from any satanic strongholds, "For though we walk in the flesh, we do not war after the flesh: For the weapons of our warfare are not carnal, but mighty through God to the pulling down of strong holds" (II Corinthians 10:3-4).

Jesus is aware that His kingdom will face corruption from the evil one, so we must be ready as well. Our God will strengthen and bring renewal to His children. May we fervently pray for deliverance and revival in our heart, home, and our nation. Jesus will grant us peace as we uproot the weeds and focus on the harvest He has for us.

Blessing and Favor on the Way

May the Lord God of your fathers make you a thousand times so many more as you are, and bless you, as he has promised you!"

Deuteronomy 1:11

Moses was reminding the Israelites what God had done for them and urging them to rededicate their lives to Him. God often needs to remind us too of how quickly we can forget the miracles and blessings He has done for us and of His faithful promises. We need to be reminded so we can rededicate ourselves to Him as well.

Although we have seen miracles, we can sometimes forget them. We tend to complain when we are tasked with something that seems impossible. This is why we should remember that Jesus is God and that we are only humans who seldom comprehend His ways. Our human nature wants to focus on the negatives or difficult circumstances in our lives. In those moments we often find ourselves forgetting everything that Jesus has done for us. Not only did He come to this world as a man and give His life to save us from sin, but He has also promised many blessings to all who follow Him.

Jesus wants to remind us of how blessed we are. When we look back over our own life, we can recognize so many blessings and how He has given us a thousand times more than we deserve. He desires to release favor and blessing into our lives and to do us good. We serve a wonderful Lord whose loving favor lasts for a lifetime and for all eternity. No matter how many blessings we expect from Jesus, His infinite kindness and generosity will always exceed all our expectations. Today, we should open our heart and mind with an attitude of expectancy, for God's blessings are coming our way!

Rejoice, the Victory is Won

This is the day which the Lord has made; we will rejoice and be glad in it.

Psalm 118:24

Each day, we should arise with an attitude of thanksgiving, filled with confident expectation of what Jesus has planned not only for our day, but also for our lives. Although everything may not be perfect currently, and we may have problems to deal with, we can decide to exalt the Lord rather than magnifying our troubles.

We can be glad in that Jesus is with us and that He will never forsake us! Rejoice because He will supply all our needs according to His riches in glory! Rejoice for He has prepared a place for us to live with Him eternally in Heaven. This is a great day to be alive and to be walking with Jesus!

Faith in God does not keep us from encountering difficulties and trials, but it does enable us to bear tribulations courageously and to emerge victoriously. Let us rejoice and be exceedingly glad! King Jesus still reigns, and everything is going to be alright! He will fight our battles. Our God never fails! We are victorious, more than conquerors through Christ Jesus our Lord! May we take our stand on the Rock of Ages. Let the battle rage; the victory is God's and ours through Him!

Pursued by God

Surely goodness and mercy shall follow me all the days of my life: and I will dwell in the house of the Lord forever.

Psalm 23:6

The author of Psalm 23, David, was recognized as a man after God's own heart. Because of his passion for God and desire to do His will, goodness and mercy followed him all the day long. The word "follow" means "to chase, to pursue." As we chase after Jesus, He will surely chase after us with His goodness and mercy!

Our Lord has much more favor and blessing stored up for us than we could ever dream. We should be living with an expectant attitude of faith. Anticipate that something good is about to happen everywhere we go and with everything we do,for God's goodness is chasing after us! His loving kindness and blessings are pursuing us! With an attitude like this, we can be certain that we will overcome any obstacles in our way and accomplish more than we can imagine. "This I know; for God is for me" (Psalm 56:9).

We are children of the Most High God! Jesus has crowned us with His loving favor. As we look behind us, we do not see our failures or the devil chasing us. No! What do we see? We see Jesus following hard after us with His goodness and mercy! Our faithful Heavenly Father daily loads us with benefits of blessing, favor, opportunity, protection, and supernatural power and strength!

Looking in the rearview mirror we see Jesus following after us with His goodness and mercy! He is with us every second of this life. He was with us yesterday. He is with us today. He will be with us tomorrow. He will be with us for all eternity!

Fresh Mercy and Compassion

It is of the Lord's mercies that we are not consumed, because his compassions fail not. They are new every morning: great is thy faithfulness.

Acts 20:24

God is merciful and His mercies are new every morning. No failure, offense, or sin is beyond His unfathomable mercy. His mercy and compassion exceed human comprehension. Our perfect, holy God cares for sinners like us...simply astounding!

Sometimes, it can be difficult to comprehend His amazing love for us. We often allow our circumstances to determine how loved we feel. However, the love Jesus has for us never ends. His love is not dependent on circumstances being good or bad, nor determined by how good we are. Life with Jesus is a succession of fresh starts and new beginnings. We are never bound to our past. We arise each morning just as fresh and clean as a newly opened spring flower.

The mercy and compassion of Jesus sustains us through the night and upholds us through the day. His mercy enables us to achieve and even thrive in life. Every single day He brings a fresh supply of mercy and compassion! We should open our hearts to receive His mercy and forgiveness. Allow Him to wash over us with His refreshing peace and joy. Then determine to share that mercy toward others.

Great is Thy faithfulness, O God my Father! There is no shadow of turning with Thee;
Thou changest not, Thy compassions, they fail not As Thou hast been Thou forever wilt be.
Great is Thy faithfulness! Great is Thy faithfulness! Morning by morning new mercies I see;
All I have needed Thy hand hath provided Great is Thy faithfulness, Lord, unto me! (Thomas Chisholm).

Our Great Reward

Cast not away therefore your confidence, which has great recompense of reward.

Hebrews 1035

During tough times in life our confidence in God and His Word are tested. Such experiences are inescapable. However, if we will continue to walk in faith, believing and trusting in Jesus, all the promises of His Word become available to us. He promises great reward!

Often the promise takes longer than anticipated. God's children frequently miss out on God's best by giving up just before their answer comes. Our faith can never take a break when we struggle through the belly of hell, so do not cast it off! Keep pressing forward in the name of Jesus!

Keep putting one foot before the other, trusting that Jesus will provide the strength needed to take one more step, …and then another, …and then another. Regardless of how hard things are presently, determine not to give in to despair. Never give up! Keep holding on to Jesus, for He is still holding on to us! Whatever we have been waiting for, keep on trusting and believing. Our answer is on the way. The promise is closer than we even realize. Although the situation may appear worse than ever, let this be a sign that we are close to our victory. Jesus is faithful and He will not fail!

Do not cast away our confidence, for our great reward is almost here! We have come too far for far too long to give up now! Let us resolve to wait patiently and confidently for the promise of our great reward and let the joy of salvation shine in our hearts daily.

Make Jesus the Main Priority

And you shall seek me, and find me, when you shall search for me with all your heart.

Jeremiah 29:13

Spending time with Jesus should be our main priority daily. Our quality of life is directly correlated with the quality of time we spend with Him.

Our time with God can easily become interrupted or replaced by "urgent" matters because we assume He will always be there. However, if we continue to ignore Him, eventually Jesus becomes an afterthought in our day, leaving him with the leftovers of our lives. We can gradually lose our closeness to Him by avoiding Him. Jesus must be our number one priority!

If we will simply focus on Jesus and keeping Him first place, then circumstances seem to fall into their right place. Putting Him first enables us to live victoriously, filled with His joy, peace, and love. Make sure our activities and attitudes align with what pleases the Lord above all others, including ourselves. What we focus our attention on the most becomes the guiding force in our lives.

May Jesus bless us with undivided hearts, ones that seek Him as the main priority. Ask Him to forgive us for allowing other things to distract our attention from Him and for people and things which we have allowed to interfere with our devotion to His kingdom. May God birth in us a holy passion for His will above all other responsibilities and interests.

Seeing God's Goodness

I had fainted unless I had believed to see the goodness of the Lord in the land of the living..

Psalm 27:13

Hope in his God soothed David's weary spirit. Heavenly hope renewed his mind, calmed his emotions, and restored his fainting heart. David resolved that, even if an enemy host encamped against him, he would not fear, and his confidence in God would stand strong.

Currently, individuals' hearts are fearful of what is happening in the world. We should pray that we can be like David, "a man after God's own heart," and maintain our trust in Jesus, even with the difficult circumstances we are facing. Realize that in His goodness, God will provide for us and protect us as He has promised. Speak words of faith now, "I am not worried or upset. I am confident in Jesus that, although my circumstances are tough, I will not allow them to steal my hope in God! His favor is coming my way!" Regardless of how bad things may seem, be confident that we will see the goodness of our Lord! He is all-powerful, Omniscient, and Creator of the universe, and He holds us in His loving hand. Nothing is too difficult for Jesus. Hold to this truth by faith!

Since we are not of this world, we should never feel hopeless, for our faith is in Jesus, the same God whom David relied upon. We also have great hope in the God of our salvation. We honor Jesus when we wholeheartedly believe His Word and trust that He is our God! He rewards those who diligently seek Him and obey Him out of love for Him. Hold fast to the joy that is set before us and watch and wait for that blessed hope and the glorious appearing of our great God and Savior, Jesus Christ!

Come Out from Among Them

Wherefore come out from among them, and be ye separate, saith the Lord, and touch not the unclean thing; and I will receive you.

II Corinthians 6:17

With this verse Paul was not calling Christians to be isolationists when rebuking the Corinthians for their worldly ways. He was warning us against worldly alliances that have a negative impact on our Christian walk and engaging in friendships that drag us away from God and into spiritual impurity.

We should never be yoked to any person or organization that does not have faith in the Lord Jesus Christ. For what partnership does righteousness have with iniquity? What fellowship has light with darkness? What accord has Christ with Satan? What agreement has our temple with the temple of idols? We are God's temple, the temple of the living God! Therefore, He commands us to come out from among them, and be separate from them, and touch nothing unclean. Then, our God will receive us, and will be a Father to us, and we will be His sons and daughters.

Determine not to settle for mediocrity, by trying to go along with the world just to get along and to be accepted. Be the individuals of excellence before the world that Jesus has called us to be. So, what if we are different. We should never compromise our loyalty and commitment to Him! We are not here to please people; we are here to please Jesus above everyone else!

Ask the Lord to cleanse us from any defilement of the body and spirit, and make His holiness perfect in us. Ask Jesus to forgive us of the sinful failure of trying to please and appease people over pleasing Him. May He empower us to grow ever closer to His character and holiness. Decide to live a holy life that attracts others to Jesus, so they may desire to follow Him too. May the Lord help us to conquer our weaknesses and to be shining lights before the world. Jesus refuses to leave us the way we are, He wants us to be just like Him!

Love the Way Jesus Loves

For in Jesus Christ neither circumcision avails anything, nor uncircumcision; but faith which works by love.

Galatians 5:6

Paul reminds us of what is essential, faith revealed in loving actions. Jesus wants our faith to express itself in vibrant and loving service. The mark of genuine faith is not adherence to a set of rules, laws, or rituals, it is LOVE for one another. Ultimately it comes down to how we express our faith. Whatever outwardly religious acts we do means nothing unless it is done out of a true heart of love towards God and others.

We can easily become caught up in our list of things to do each day. We may even have a list of spiritual things we want to accomplish daily, like reading the Bible and praying, to please Jesus. Of course, it is important for us to want to please God; yet, pleasing Him begins with the condition of the heart. The Bible informs us that only our faith, hope, and love will never fail us. Make certain we are not simply going through the motions of our spiritual walk. We may have great knowledge and accomplish many good tasks, but without love, it will not matter. If love is the basis for everything we speak and do, Jesus will empower us to live victoriously, and His favor and blessings will overtake us.

Choose love, knowing that it energizes our faith. We do not want to be guilty of simply going through the motions of being a Christian. May the Lord forgive us for the times we have lost sight of what is essential, for the times our interests and concerns were more important to us than loving service to others. May Jesus give us eyes to see the people He would have us serve daily so others may know His love. Desire to love the way Jesus loves us. May He reveal to us ways to grow in love as we keep our heart and mind set on Him.

Praising Our Way to Peace

Be careful for nothing; but in everything by prayer and supplication with thanksgiving let your requests be made known unto God. And the peace of God, which passes all understanding, shall keep your hearts and minds through Christ Jesus.

Philippians 4:6-7

Jesus cannot give us happiness and peace apart from Himself. There is no such thing. Many people are trying to make peace, yet this has already been done. Jesus has not left it for us to do. All we need to do is to enter into His peace. The key to living in peace is to "Enter into His gates with thanksgiving and into His courts with praise: be thankful unto him, and bless his name" (Psalm 100:4). He desires to hear and receive our prayers. To prevent them from being too self-centered, God asks us to always give thanks.

We can easily turn prayer into a wish list. The absence of praise and thanksgiving with our prayers leaves them lacking or empty. Leaving off praise causes our hearts to darken, because all we consider is our problems, then prayer becomes a request line. When we release all our worries and fears to Jesus in prayer and praise, we gain a new perspective in which He becomes magnified in our eyes and our problems become smaller and less significant. He replaces our fears with hope, peace, joy, and love.

We cannot be at peace with others if we are not at peace with ourselves. We cannot be at peace with ourselves if we are not at peace with Jesus. Resign every forbidden joy and restrain from every wish that is not considered God's will. Discard all eager desires, all anxiety, and desire only the will of God. Seek Him alone and supremely, and we will find peace. Genuine peace must come from within. "We cannot change or control the world around us, but we can change and control the world within ourselves" (Warren Wiersbe). Only when we have peace within ourselves can we bring peace to others.

Busy Waiting, Busy Loving Jesus

If we hope for that we see not, then do we with patience wait for it.

Romans 8:25

We may consider ourselves to not be very good at waiting. However, our hope and trust in Jesus provide us with patience beyond human inclination. We can be completely confident that the good things Jesus has in store for us is beyond our imaginations and what He has promised will come to pass.

In the midst of any circumstance Jesus wants us to stay positive, hopeful, and guided by our faith in Him and His Word. Faith allows us to believe things that may not even seem rational to our carnal minds. Walking by faith does not mean we ignore our situation or the circumstances. It means we decide to focus our attention on Jesus, trusting that He is greater than everything we are going through, and that He will "do exceedingly abundantly above all that we ask or think, according to the power that works in us" (Ephesians 3:20).

In these uncertain times, learn to trust God's Word over any fear and doubt, and declare words of faith to each circumstance. Faith allows us to believe the unbelievable. Hope causes us to hope when all seems hopeless. Faith's reward is seeing what we believe. While we wait patiently, try to stay busy…busy loving God and sharing His mercy and truth with others.

Patiently Hope and Pray

Rejoicing in hope; patient in tribulation; continuing instant in prayer.

Romans 12:12

Do we consider ourselves to be patient? Our demanding lives, with both big and small concerns, require us to utilize patience routinely. Initiating patience is usually much easier said than done. However, our greatest blessings will come with patience.

We cannot control all facets of our lives. How people speak to and behave toward us are frequently outside our ability to control; so, we search for ways to cope with and survive them. Scripture tells us how to be patient through difficult circumstances—rejoice in hope and be constant in prayer. We may not understand the waiting period, but we can hope and pray in realizing that Jesus controls our lives and is turning challenging situations for our good. Instead of attempting to cause things to happen a certain way, we can release the reigns and give our Heavenly Father all the authority to work on our behalf.

When we place our trust in Jesus and His perfect plan rather than our own, we never have to feel fearful, worried, or impatient. His plan is better than anything we could imagine. Be patient and keep the faith during times when life is challenging, and everything seems to work against us. Jesus blesses those who hope, pray, and endure, who patiently wait and trust in His powerful deliverance. May Jesus continue to give us patience and assurance that He will never fail to keep His Word.

Faith Born in Despair

Now faith is the substance of things hoped for, the evidence of things not seen.

Hebrews 11:1

According to this Scripture, faith is the evidence of things not seen. There are promises in the Bible that we cannot always see with our physical eyes. Even though we cannot see these promises, we believe them to be true.

Falling into negativity seems effortless, when others are fearful all around us and circumstances appear dreary at best. Fear is the antonym and complete opposite to faith. Faith does not look at what is happening to us, rather it centers on Jesus in Whom we trust and with Whom anything is possible. Faith makes life bearable with all its struggles and uncertainties. The best way for us to grow to great faith is by enduring great trials. Our responsibility is to keep trusting Jesus while He continually works on our behalf.

The ultimate treasures of life must be fought for and won. Keep moving forward! Never give up! Our hardest struggles will lead to the greatest moments of our lives. Challenging situations develop strong people in the end. Rest assured, there is never a moment when our God is not in control. So, stay calm! Jesus has our back! The greatest faith is birthed in the hour of despair. When we can see no hope and no way out, then faith arises and brings the victory! Thank You Jesus!

Work Hard for Success

But you shall remember the Lord your God: for it is he who gives you power to get wealth...

Deuteronomy 8:18

We often can think we deserve all the good that happens to us, yet easily forget to thank the Lord when life is good. Plus, in hard times, it becomes even easier for us to murmur and complain and even blame God for letting it happen. Remember, every blessing comes from Him and not necessarily because we deserve it. All we have and all we are is only by His mercy and grace.

Jesus has prepared promises and blessings that our mind has not yet even fathomed. God grants us the power to obtain wealth. "Wealth" is having abundance and success. If we are willing and obedient, living a godly and sanctified life of integrity, we will experience His promise of blessings being poured out upon our lives. Just as a tree planted by the water, our leaf shall not wither, and whatsoever we do will prosper!

God gives the power and ability to get wealth. He causes us to be innovative and creative with ideas, but our responsibility is to do all we can diligently, to the best of our ability (see Ecclesiastes 9:10). The difference between success and failure is work. God will not do what we can and should do for ourselves. If we will do our best, God will do the rest!

Deep down, we realize we do not deserve all the goodness God has given, although we sometimes think we have earned it. May Jesus forgive us for thinking this way. A powerful key to success is to never make excuses. Success results from maximum utilization of our abilities to the glory of God. "The foundation stones for a balanced success are honesty, character, integrity, faith, love and loyalty" (Zig Ziglar).

Never Is Forever

…I will never leave you, nor forsake you.

Hebrews 13:5

Our primary decision daily is either to live by faith or by sight. Trust in God's promises and power or rely upon our own resources. However, our abilities and resources are limited, while His are limitless. Ours are easily spent, while His never runs out. Jesus is always present and dependable for us. He is the only one who will NEVER leave nor forsake us! Never is forever, and this one never we treasure.

If we are facing difficulty, trust Jesus and remember that He is with us always, every step of the way, and through it all. He never said that we would not have any problems, but He did say that we would never face them alone. He is continually working all things together for our good to give us an expected end.

Jesus protects us from becoming too worldly, draws us closer to Him, teaches us patience, increases our faith, and so much more. During tough times let us take hold of Jesus Christ, the Rock which can never be moved "The Lord is my rock, and my fortress, and my deliverer; my God, my strength, in whom I will trust; my buckler, and the horn of my salvation, and my high tower" (Psalm 18:2). When we trust Jesus through everything, He secures us and fills us with more of Him—more of His love, more of His joy, and more of His peace. "I have set the Lord always before me: because he is at my right hand, I shall not be moved" (Psalm 16:8).

Praise the Lord for always being there, in our past, present, and future. Jesus is present even when we are unaware of Him. May He give us courage to truly believe His promises, especially His promise to never leave us alone.

God Calls It Like He Sees It

...God, who quickens the dead, and calls those things which be not as though they were.

Romans 4:17

God gives life to the dead and He calls those things which do not exist as though they did. He views death as sleep. Nothing is ever impossible or too difficult for Him. Just as He raised Lazarus and Jairus's daughter from the dead, Jesus still performs miracles out of impossible situations.

Jesus can bring people and things to life physically, emotionally, and spiritually—mental disorders, finances, broken relationships, addictions, manic depressants, or the spiritually dead. He desires to resurrect situations which seem impossible and breathe life into them. Regardless of how hopeless a situation appears; no situation is too dead when it is surrendered to Jesus. If He can raise the dead and create life out of Sarah's lifeless womb, He can create life in any struggle we are dealing with.

Jesus does not call us what we are. He calls us the way He sees us. He creates with His words. He sees us as well able, having what it takes, and strong in Him. Although we may often feel weak, insecure, and inferior, we can do all things through Christ Jesus! His promise may not materialize overnight; but gradually he is molding and shaping us into His image and toward fulfilling our divine calling. Be strong, bold, and confident in the Most High God!

Call things that are not as though they are. Call things as we see them through eyes of faith! Instead of using our words to complain about our situation, use them to help change and improve it! Continue speaking words of faith. Keep praying, believing, and pressing forward to the promising future Jesus has in store!

Triumphant Faith Conquers Fear

There is no fear in love; but perfect love casts out fear...

I John 4:18

Fear can be a self-imposed prison, keeping us from becoming who and what God desires for us. Fear is the major weapon the enemy uses to prevent us from progressing and enjoying the blessed life God has for us. Satan does everything in his power trying to take our focus away from our loving and faithful God. Loving Jesus is the antidote to fear and worry.

Conquer fear with weapons of faith and love. Love for Jesus immunizes us from the harmful and painful symptoms brought about by fear. The presence of love for and hope in the invincible sovereignty of God drives out fear. No matter what we are facing, Jesus is greater than our worries, problems, and fears. He knows our every need and delights in caring for us.

The chains of love are more powerful and stronger than the chains of fear. "The Lord is my light and my salvation; whom shall I fear? the Lord is the strength of my life; of whom shall I be afraid?" (Psalm 27:1). When we are filled with faith, Satan is filled with fear. Let us keep our faith strong each day, so we can keep our enemy fearful of us. "Yea, though I walk through the valley of the shadow of death, I will fear no evil: for thou art with me; thy rod and thy staff they comfort me" (Psalm 23:4). We have triumphant faith in the name of Jesus!

Creative Power of the Spoken Word

...Now, I beseech you, let the power of my lord be great, according as you have spoken...

Numbers 14:17

God created the whole universe through His spoken word. When He came to Earth as a man, He spoke and commanded the wind and the sea to be still, and they immediately obeyed His voice. Jesus simply spoke and healed the leper and delivered a man from horrible demon possession. As children of the Most High God, we also have creative power in our words.

Jesus said, "...Verily I say unto you, If you have faith as a grain of mustard seed, you shall say unto this mountain, Remove hence to yonder place; and it shall remove; and nothing shall be impossible unto you" (Matthew 17:20). We set the course of our day and our world with our words. "Death and life are in the power of the tongue..." (Proverbs 18:21). We can declare an atmosphere of peace, joy, love, wellness, and power with our words, or we can create an atmosphere of strife, chaos, and pessimism.

Now is the time to use our words as they were intended, to open the door of our lives wide for Jesus to operate fully, by declaring scriptural promises of strength and victory. No enemy can defeat us, and no weapon formed against us will prosper! We are more than conquerors though Christ Jesus our Lord! Nothing shall separate us from His love, His joy, and His peace! We declare this to be so, in the name of Jesus!

Love Like Jesus

Love your enemies, do good to them which hate you, Bless them that curse you, and pray for them which despitefully use you...And as you would that men should do to you, do you also to them likewise

Luke 6:27-28, 31

Many individuals want us to do as they say, even though they do not even do what they say. Jesus loved the unlovable, forgave those who misused and abused Him, and even forgive those who crucified Him. He is the perfect example of tender, sacrificial, and radical love expressed beyond human comprehension.

Love includes a redemptive, life-transforming power. Being compassionate and loving in heart and deeds toward our enemies is never easy. Jesus fills us with love by His Spirit, for "...The love of God has been shed abroad in our hearts by the Holy Ghost which is given unto us" (Romans 5:5). Jesus empowers us to love unconditionally, just like Him! Our love can even rescue our enemies from their hate toward us.

If we are experiencing trouble from someone at work, school, or within our families, who seem adamantly intent on criticizing, undermining, belittling, and trying to defeat us, treat this unlovable person the way we want to be treated. "Do unto others as you would have them do unto you." As we apply the loving, caring character of Jesus, we will be able to resist their attacks and be filled with immeasurable joy, love, and peace. May we love and forgive like Jesus.

Sacred Urgency for Pending Deadline

That the trial of your faith, being much more precious than of gold that perishes, though it be tried with fire, might be found unto praise and honor and glory at the appearing of Jesus Christ.

I Peter 4:7

We behave differently from people around us when we know a deadline is near—a term paper for school, a work project, or a candid conversation with a friend or family member. Deadlines cause us to sharpen our focus, see what is most valuable, and act resolutely. Jesus wants us to live each moment and perceive every encounter with someone with sacred urgency.

In our relationship with Jesus, we are to live with heartfelt commitment and discipline in our prayer life, for He is our only real answer. In our relationships with one another in God's family, we are to demonstrate unwavering love, for love enables us to keep moving forward, despite our flaws and scars.

We do not know when our appointed time to leave this Earth will occur. Neither do we know the precise day nor time when Jesus will return for His bride, the Church. However, He expects us to live with urgency and preparedness, realizing that many people around us are running out of time and opportunity to come to Him. People need to be able to look at us and perceive that we have been with Jesus. Our life should help draw others to Jesus, especially from our genuine love and concern for them.

Today is the day of salvation! May we be intentional and have a sense of sacred urgency in being ready for the greatest ever approaching deadline and in reaching others for Jesus.

Turn the Page

Your eyes did see my substance, yet being imperfect; and in your book all my members were written, which in continuance were fashioned, when as yet there was none of them.

Psalm 139:16

God in His perfect omniscience knows everything about our lives in advance. The Lord saw our unborn state and planned the days we would live. He has already written our life's story with plans for our good, to prosper us and to give us peace. "For I know the thoughts that I think toward you, saith the Lord, thoughts of peace, and not of evil, to give you an expected end" (Jeremiah 29:11). We may still face challenging situations, but Jesus will use all we go through to lead us onward in His good plan.

At times, we may question God when bad things happen. Do not allow circumstances which we do not immediately understand to cause us to become trapped on the same page in our life's story. Determine to keep turning the page so that we can experience each victory awaiting us in each new chapter. Jesus plans to turn every circumstance around for our ultimate good. Our life's story is not over! Keep journeying onward and upward! Keep trusting and believing! Keep our hopes and dreams alive! Now is the time to turn the page and see the favor and blessing Jesus has in store!

Jesus is intricately involved in our life. He even knows the number of hairs on our head. He is fully aware of all our problems and knows our desires and dreams. Praise Him for being God, Lord, and King of kings! He knew us before we came forth from our mother's womb, and He knows our limited time on this Earth. Trust Him to order our life and to lead us all the way to the Promised Land—our final destination and eternal home in Heaven!

Never Too Good to Be True

He did not waver at the promise of God through unbelief; but was strong in faith, giving glory to God.

Romans 4:20

Abraham was unwavering regarding God's promises, in spite of his impossible circumstances. God had promised that he and his wife, Sarah, would have a child, even though they were far past childbearing years. How did Abraham handle the situation? He became "strong in faith, giving glory to God!" He was faithful and glorified the Lord for he knew his promised son would come and that God was faithful to keep His Word. He continued praising the Lord for what was engrained in his heart and soul. God's promise to him was ultimately fulfilled.

Faith involves trusting in the future promises of God and waiting for their fulfillment. We too should praise and give God glory while we wait for His promises. Although we may be in an impossible situation beyond our control, Jesus will not fail to keep His Word. He has spoken promises deep in our hearts, and we know that we know that we know, that what our God has spoken, He will bring to pass. What He has started, He will finish.

Allow God's promises to shine on our problems. Continue to be strong and grow in faith as we wait on the Lord. Keep seeking Him in prayer, trusting and anticipating His fulfilled promises in our lives. Choose to adore, exalt, and glorify Jesus despite our challenging circumstances. God's Word is full of promises to us–promises filled with hope and eternal life. And Jesus doesn't lie, so that means that every promise He has ever made is coming true. If we are worried, scared, or hurting, pray and meditate on His Word for lasting encouragement and remind ourselves of the good promises of God. Jesus never made a promise too good to be true!

Declare New Things for Our Life

Behold, the former things are come to pass, and new things do I declare:
before they spring forth I tell you of them

Isaiah 42:9

God promises new things will come into our life. If we will open our heart to Him and ask Him to reveal to us what He would have us to do, the kind of person He wants us to be, and where He would have us go, He will show Himself strong in us and will exceed our expectations. He will enable us to experience new things while our "inward man is renewed day by day" (II Corinthians 4:16).

Be on the lookout for the new things Jesus desires to show us. Remain alert. Listen to His voice as He speaks to us through Scripture and guides us by His Spirit. Anticipate the new things He will do that will simply amaze us. Open our heart and expand our vision to whatever the Lord has planned.

Jesus wants to show us new things. Are we ready to see something new in our life? The Bible tells us that "death and life are in the power of the tongue" (Proverbs 18:21). This means we greatly influence our future according to what we speak. If we need to see change in our situation, then start by changing our words. Instead of using our words to describe our circumstance, speak words to help change it. Declare new things to start seeing new things! Proclaim blessing, declare joy, speak wellness and success. Proclaim Gods scriptural promises and watch Him shape our future and guide us into wonderful new things!

Unutterable Prayers

Likewise the Spirit also helps our infirmities: for we know not what we should pray for as we ought: but the Spirit itself makes intercession for us with groanings which cannot be uttered.

Romans 8:26

Sometimes the deepest yearnings of the heart are concealed within. We may not even understand what our hidden hopes or deepest wounds are, but they become a longing in our soul, an unquenchable thirst. This is when the Holy Spirit will intervene in our limitations by interceding on our behalf.

Our God is so amazing! When we cannot even find the words to speak and our heart feels extremely heavy, Jesus hears our prayers. His Spirit dwelling within expresses and makes known what our words cannot verbalize and what our mind cannot fathom. Jesus hears the longing and cry from our heart. He understands all that we think and feel. He answers our unutterable prayers as we allow the Spirit to intercede through us with "groanings which cannot be uttered."

Jesus takes our rawest and deepest prayers and perfects them through the manifest presence of His Spirit! Then He answers them in the best possible way. Therefore, we should always pray until the Spirit takes control of our prayers and flows mightily through intercession. Our heart then becomes completely yielded to "Thy will be done!"

We are comforted by the assurance that, even if we do not know what to say, the Spirit of God within knows what we are unable to communicate. Trust Jesus to answer our yearnings as He thinks best, for He knows what we need more than we know how to ask for it. Thank Him for knowing our heart better than we know ourselves. May He take our inner thirsts and longings and beautify them, so our life will glorify Him. Praise Him for the blessed assurance that the power of our prayers is not dependent upon our words but upon His Holy Spirit's intercession!

Making Something of Our Nothing

And the earth was without form, and void; and darkness was upon the
face of the deep. And the Spirit of God moved upon the face of the waters.
And God said, Let there be light: and there was light.

Genesis 1:2-3

God made the entire universe out of nothing. He spoke it into existence. If we need a miracle regarding something seemingly impossible, know that we serve the Omnipotent, all-powerful God, who can create anything out of nothing!

Jesus makes a way where there seems to be no way and opens opportunities which seem forever closed! If He made all this out of nothing, then He can take any emptiness in our lives and make it wonderful and lovely too. The Lord can take our weakness, failure, emptiness, and nothingness that we have to offer Him and make it into something magnificent that will glorify Him. He will speak light into our darkest hour, give shape to our formless hopes and dreams, revive our lost talents, and make our crooked places straight! He can do this because He is God!

Take hold of His promise of life and purpose. Proclaim life to our shattered dreams and lost hopes. Let faith arise and confidently anticipate that Jesus will turn our situation and circumstances around in our favor, creating something out of nothing! "I will praise you; for I am fearfully and wonderfully made: marvelous are your works; and that my soul knows right well" (Psalm 139:14).

Greater Glory Is on the Way

The glory of this latter house shall be greater than of the former, says the Lord of hosts.

Haggai 2:9

God's house is not made of bricks and mortar, neither can it be made by man. His house is made up of Christian believers. Jesus wants to turn this house into a home, as He dwells in our heart daily, making us greater! "…Know you not that your body is the temple of the Holy Ghost…" (I Corinthians 6:19). The great mystery is "…Christ in you the hope of glory" (Colossians 1:27).

Our future looks bright and will be better than our present. God is with us, and He never fails. When Jesus is with us, all the strength and ability we will ever need is with us. Do not worry about how things will turn out. Our circumstances will be different, and they will be better, because we will be better!

We have only touched the surface of all that Jesus has awaiting us. He desires to make us better and to give us greater, for "…Greater is He that is in you than he that is in the world" (I John 4:4). The blessing and favor of our past and present have been amazing, but our God is going to top this. He is a God of increase Who has much more in store for our future!

We may not look like much on the outside to the world, yet Jesus is beautifying the inside to prepare us for blessing and opportunity. The glory of this latter house shall be greater than the former! We are about to experience a fresher and deeper relationship with Jesus than ever before! Expand our vision! We can do all things through Christ Jesus, and with Him anything is possible! Our future glory and blessing are just around corner!

Praise Our Way to Victory

But thanks be to God, who gives us the victory through our Lord Jesus Christ.

I Corinthians 15:57

Jesus desires to give us His favor so we may live victoriously. He will always give us the victory, regardless of what we face. Abundant and eternal life is ours! Sin and death no longer enslave us! We are victorious through Jesus Christ our Lord. All that is left to be said is "Praise God!"

The greatest faith is birthed during the hour of despair. When things seem hopeless, with no way out, then faith rises and brings the victory. Though we be fraught with sickness or pain, healing is ours. Although we may be heartbroken—peace, emotional wellbeing, and restoration are ours to claim. Even if we have strayed from the Lord, He desires to grant forgiveness and spiritual restoration. Anything we need, in God's favor we have provision and all our needs supplied according to His riches in glory.

Murmuring and complaining about our present circumstances will only result in us becoming trapped in an unpleasant situation longer. However, if we praise Jesus in the midst of our trial, He will cause us to triumph over it. "Outlook determines outcome. If we see only the problems, we will be defeated; but if we see the possibilities in the problems, we can have victory" (Warren Wiersbe). Open the door for victory right now by offering thanksgiving, praise, adoration, and worship to the Most High God! Magnify Jesus rather than our problems!

Forever Changed

Therefore I take pleasure in infirmities, in reproaches, in necessities, in persecutions, in distresses for Christ's sake: for when I am weak, then am I strong.

II Corinthians 12:10

Paul suffered greatly as a Christian. He was beaten, stoned, shipwrecked, arrested, and imprisoned time and again. Yet, through everything he continued walking with and trusting in Jesus. From his experiences, we realize that each trial we endure manifests the strength of Jesus in our lives. The Spirit and power of Jesus gives us strength to stand, even in the most difficult times. Therefore, we can "take pleasure in infirmities, in reproaches, in necessities, in persecutions, in distresses for Christ's sake: for when I am weak, then am I strong!"

From Scripture, we realize anything can happen anytime and anywhere. The Bible prepares us to face our trials. Each of us have survived experiences that felt unbearable, yet we made it through. Praise God! We are still standing! The scars and memories from those struggles are our testimonies and proof of God's very existence. Whatever difficulty we may be facing now, declare, "I shall not die, but live, and declare the works of the LORD" (Psalm 118:17).

Scripture gives us the encouragement we need! Keep holding on to Jesus, and worship Him through the tears and pain. He has put a song in our heart, His grace has brought us safe thus far; and His grace will lead us home! By God's grace, we realize all that happens can draw us ever closer to Jesus.

Our trials reveal the strength of Jesus if we remain faithful to Him and continue walking with Him. Although we may feel weak and tired, know that His strength upholds us. We are forever changed with each trial we endure. Yet, through His grace and provision, Jesus binds our wounds, heals our brokenness, and restores our peace and joy.

Praise God for healing and restoration as we live with our scars. May we see our scars as testimonies of His grace and strength, as Jesus works in our lives to draw us nearer to Him and to give us much needed strength and courage.

Nuturing Faith

So then faith cometh by hearing, and hearing by the word of God.

Romans 10:17

The Bible informs us that everyone has been given a measure of faith. Faith can develop and grow, but it can also be reduced and weakened. Faith is activated when we hear God's Word. Faith grows and increases as we obey Scripture and walk in its truth. The more we hear and say "yes" to scriptural Truth, the more unbelief and doubt fades away. God's Truth makes us free, and our faith becomes stronger.

Our faith must be watered by God's Spirit and fertilized by His Word daily to grow, just as a seed needs water and sunshine to grow. Read the Bible, meditate on and memorize Scripture each day. Speak the Word and read it again and again, in order to internalize it. His truth will take deep root in our heart and soul and prepare us for every circumstance and situation in life.

Living with passionate faith is essential to living an abundant life. Jesus is faithful no matter what, but faith allows us to have trust in His faithfulness, producing peace and calm during all life's challenges, something we desperately need today. May our faith be stirred as we meditate on the biblical principle that faith comes by hearing. May the pages of Scripture guide us to a lifestyle of trust, hope, and surrender. Finally, may we experience the joy of living by faith in response to the amazing acts of the faithfulness of Jesus Christ our Lord.

Lifegiving Favor

*For his anger endures but a moment; in his favor is life: weeping may
endure for a night, but joy comes in the morning*

Psalm 30:5

Jesus is the God of all comfort. Even when He chastens us
for our sin and rebellion, He does it for our good. The pain
from His reprimand only lasts for a short time, then He turns
our sorrow into rejoicing and sets our heart to dancing with a
renewed joyful song!

If we are experiencing discipline or encountering harsh
consequences from sin, do not despair, for joy comes in the
morning! For the called according to God's divine purpose, His
anger always turns to His favor anytime we humble ourselves
and return to Him. Momentary chastening will continuously be
transformed into grace. Weeping may undeniably endure for a
night, but joy comes in the morning. God's favor will dawn,
and it is certainly worth the wait!

When we choose to put Jesus first and obey His
commands, He opens doors for His favor, which allows us to
have an advantage for success! Our greatest opportunities are
on the way. Jesus is a faithful God! Keep doing right, honor
and trust Him, and He will grant His favor and blessing. He
will restore above all the enemy has stolen, for in His favor is
abundant life!

If we are facing difficulties, may Jesus help us endure
through the night, so that when His joyful dawn comes, we will
experience the great rejoicing that lies ahead. May we discover
His joy with each new dawn. Thank Him that despite what
problems and pain we go through in this life, our weeping will
be replaced with laughter and pain with unspeakable joy and
full of glory!

Glory in the Cross

But now is Christ risen from the dead and become the firstfruits of them that slept...even so in Christ shall all be made alive.

I Corinthians 15:20 & 22

Jesus Christ is risen indeed! Because He is risen, we no longer abide in sin. His resurrection is irrefutable proof that all our sins have been fully forgiven. By way of faith in His finished work at Calvary, we have received the gift of salvation. We do not deserve this gift, nor could we ever earn it. Jesus freely gave His own life to ransom ours. Hallelujah!

We are saved by grace through faith. This is the gift of God (see Ephesians 2:8-9). This is our immovable foundation, erected on the completed work of Jesus Christ our Lord. Righteousness is not just about doing right. Righteousness with Jesus is about believing right. We are made righteous in His sight when we believe and place our faith in Jesus and His sacrifice for us. We have been made righteous and justified by Him. Being justified is removing all of sin's guilt and punishment and understanding that we have been made righteous by the blood Jesus shed on the Cross.

Because of God's sacrifice, we have access to His favor, wisdom, power, and every benefit of His finished work released into our life to turn everything around for our good and for His glory. "God forbid that I should glory, save in the cross of our Lord Jesus Christ..." (Galatians 6:14). Only in the Cross of Jesus can we receive power when we are powerless. We can find strength when we are weak. We can experience hope when our situation seems hopeless. Only in the Cross of Jesus is there peace for our troubled heart and soul.

Be Glad and Rejoice

I will be glad and rejoice in your mercy: for you have considered my trouble;
you have known my soul in adversities.

Psalm 31:7

God delivered David from countless distressful circumstances, and David understood he could continuously depend on God because of His unwavering love. God saw David's difficulties and demonstrated His love through the trouble and caused David to be glad and rejoice. Despite the numerous setbacks we have experienced, God knows and loves us through it all.

Jesus sees and cares about everything that happens in our lives. He knows each of our failures as well as every wrong that has been committed against us. We may have lost a loved one to death, experienced a traumatic time in marriage, or possibly betrayed by family or friends. These and many other circumstances are what we call "trouble," which in the Hebrew is defined as "poverty" or "misery." If we have walked through any of these situations, we have truly known misery and distress of the soul, just as David describes in this verse. Yet, we will be glad and rejoice in God's love, for He has seen our affliction and knows the anguish of our soul!

During trouble and adversity, we could easily become bitter and angry and spend time living with heartache and feeling miserable. But, if we will simply turn to Jesus and cast all our cares on Him, He will restore our soul and set our heart to dancing! Jesus sees where we are; He knows where we have been; and He realizes the battles we face within and without. Release the struggle to Him. Trust Jesus to tenderly care for us. His unconditional and steadfast love and mercy will bring limitless joy to our lives!

A New Song of Praise

I waited patiently for the Lord; and he inclined unto me and heard my cry. He brought me up also out of a horrible pit, out of the miry clay, and set my feet upon a rock, ...And he has put a new song in my mouth, even praise unto our God.

Psalm 40:1-3

God has promised to be an ever-present help in times of trouble and to work all circumstances of life together for the good of those that love Him with all their heart, fit in with His plan, and do not lean on their own understanding. His help will come at just the right time. By not providing His help too soon, He allows the necessary time to deepen our faith and trust in Him and His never-failing Word. Neither does He provide help too slowly, which could cause us to become discouraged.

In the same way that God brought David out of despair, He will lift us up. Jesus will not leave us nor forsake us in the pit of despair. If we will praise and exalt Him, He will lift us up out of the horrible pit and set our feet on a solid foundation. Despite what pit of suffering and shame we may be required to endure, God promises to set our feet on the Rock of our Salvation and establish our goings out and our comings in, from this time forth even for evermore!

Wait patiently for King Jesus, knowing that His plans and purposes are perfect, for in due time He will incline His ear to our cry and graciously provide all we need, according to His riches in glory. If David fighting his enemies, running from King Saul, and hiding in mountains and caves, could sing praises to the Lord, so can we! Right now, Jesus wants to give us a new song of praise!

Our Refuge and Strength

God is our refuge and strength, a very present help in trouble.

Psalm 46:1

Our God is a safe refuge and mighty strength in whom we can feel safe during life's storms. We can always run to Him for protection amid an increasingly anti-Christian world. Regardless of how much the world rages against His people, Jesus will never leave nor forsake us. He will be our constant, ever-present help in troublesome times.

Never fear, for Jesus has already wrought the final victory. He has declared this to be so in His Word. Once He has spoken it, His Word is forever settled. We too are victorious in Him! Victory is ours in the name of Jesus! Therefore, we can stand firm in this evil day and trust we our secure in His loving presence.

Today, if we are facing trouble or adversity, know that Jesus is with us. Look to Him for help. Be still and know that Jesus is the Almighty God! He is our refuge and strength. Praise and adore Him as we stand on the solid foundation of Scripture. May we be strong and resolute against all evil influences in the world and trust in His unfailing Word. "Therefore, will not we fear, though the earth be removed, and though the mountains be carried into the midst of the sea!" (Psalm 46:2).

Ordering Our Steps

The steps of a good man are ordered by the Lord: and he delights in his way.

Psalm 37:23

Is there an area of our life where we need to stop making plans and instead decide to surrender it to God's will and direction? Jesus has a distinct purpose for each of us. Someone else will influence our life's direction if we do not allow Jesus to order our steps.

We may have stumbled our way through much of life, resulting in terribly embarrassing or even shameful occurrences. However, we can be confident in our spiritual life, even if we have stumbled from time to time, God will never allow us to be completely cast down if we will keep seeking for His path. When we start thinking we are about to plunge into the depths of the abyss, our Heavenly Father assures us of His unfailing love and compassion. Each time we turn to Scripture for guidance, Jesus keeps us from destruction and lifts us away from the abyss. He never leaves nor forsakes, and He is mighty to save!

Turn from any discouraging and distracting influences and focus on Jesus and His Word. Determine to walk in His will. Our God believes in us. If He can do anything with nothing, then He can surely make something wonderful of our lives. Thank Him for lifting us when we have been down, protecting us when we have been vulnerable, and comforting us when we have been broken. Praise Him for His grace and closeness. Thank Him for walking alongside us, for holding us firmly in the palm of His hand, for never letting go of us even when we chose to act against His will. May Jesus bring unfathomable peace as we wait patiently for His direction.

Jesus Is Calling

Deep calleth unto deep at the noise of thy waterspouts...

Psalm 42:7

The longing within our hearts today is to distance ourselves from the religious machine on the insanity cycle of religious activity and career Christianity that battles against the flow of the Spirit and the fresh move of God emerging now. This is our greatest test at this time of our lives. Will we determine to ride this powerful wave of His presence and calling, or will we become complicit with the masses by attempting to duplicate the superficial religiosity of the church? Will we remain trapped in the performance cycle and addicted to approval and acceptance, or will we cast ourselves at the feet of Jesus Christ our King to hear a fresh message from Him and to be empowered by His Spirit?

God is stirring the nest of His remnant. We may seem irrelevant to the world currently, yet a stirring in our very soul and a tugging at our heart is Jesus leading us out of the church world and its ways toward a fresh anointing and a new relationship and path with Him. We undoubtedly feel it stirring deep within! The resistance to being real with God has never been more direct and forceable. Therefore, we know, beyond the shadow of any doubt that we must pry ourselves away from surface religion and run into the safe and secure arms of Jesus! We must tear up the fallow ground and follow God's fresh new path!

Jesus is birthing something new, and He is inviting us to become part of it. The choice is ours. What will we do?

Be Like Jesus

O Lord, how great are thy works! and thy thoughts are very deep.

Psalms 92:5

God's thoughts are not our thoughts, neither are His thoughts even remotely like ours. We cannot even make a comparison. We think, "Maintain and care for the body;" He thinks, "Save the soul." We envision a pay raise and more possessions. He envisions raising the dead. We avoid pain and suffering and search for peace. Jesus uses pain to bring about peace. We determine, "I want to really live and enjoy life before I die." Jesus tells us, "Die, so you can truly live and have eternal life." We love what perishes and fades away. Jesus loves what endures. We rejoice in our achievements. He rejoices in our honesty and confessions. We show our children famous people with multi-million-dollar contracts and say, "Be like that." Jesus points to the cross that held His bloody and bruised body and says, "Be like me!"

Restore the Power

But you shall receive power, after that the Holy Ghost has come upon you...

Acts 1:8

Imagine it is the middle of winter and the electricity has been knocked out by an ice storm. As we listen to a battery-powered radio the announcer says, "The following businesses, schools, and churches will be closed due to the increment weather." This would certainly seem a rational thing to do. However, what if on a particular day an announcement was made, "The following churches will be closed due to lack of power"? What a provocative announcement! Our churches of today would most likely never be closed due to the lack of programs and activities, yet most could certainly be closed due to the lack of Holy Spirit power!

Jesus put His Spirit in us so we could be known for our power, rather known for His Power in us. Sadly, the majority of believers and churches are recognized for talent and intellect instead of supernatural power. The worst part of it is most have accepted this powerlessness as normal and okay. No doubt countless believers around the world, especially here in America, if asked, would probably admit to not having experienced the manifest presence of Jesus in their lives over the past year. Even greater sadness is they probably do not believe they can experience it. "If the Holy Spirit was withdrawn from the church today, 95 percent of what we do would go on and no one would know the difference. If the Holy Spirit had been withdrawn from the New Testament church (in Acts), 95 percent of what they did would stop, and everybody would know the difference" (A. W. Tozer).

Jesus desires for each of us to return to a fresh Pentecostal experience, like what occurred in chapter two of Acts. The cry from the depths of our very soul should be "Jesus, You are the air I breath, Your Holy Presence living in me. You are my daily bread, Your very Word spoken to me. Jesus I'm Desperate for You! I'm lost without You." If we are to be the temple of God, then God's Spirit must dwell within! May Jesus restore the POWER to our lives today!

Read the Bible

...Keep my words, and lay up my commandments with thee. Keep my commandments, and live; and my law as the apple of thine eye. Bind them upon thy fingers, write them upon the table of thine heart.

Proverbs 7:1-3

All Christians have a Bible in their home; yet the question is "How often do they read it?" Far too often we take time to watch TV, surf the Internet, or some other activity and neglect Bible reading. Reading the Scriptures can feel mundane or like an obligation instead of a blessing. However, reading our Bible can benefit us more than we could possibly realize.

If we will read God's Word, we also can acquire deeper understanding of ourselves, humanity, the world, and of God. The Bible is God's blueprint for successful living. Its principles provide the guidelines to follow if we want to receive His blessings. His Word warns us of dangers and temptations we will face and will teach us how to avoid them and to be victorious over them. Being guided by Scripture grants us wisdom to make the good decisions and to choose the right path for our lives.

Even if we do not feel like doing it, take time to read the Bible and meditate on God's Word daily. Make sure we know God's Word. Read the Bible. Study the Bible. Make it our life's foundation. Believe its promises. Follow its warnings. Keep its commands. Jesus will speak into our life and situation through Scripture. Living according to His principles opens the door to His wisdom—to receiving His power, protection, and blessing, and all that He has prepared for us!

Be Careful with Our Words

A hypocrite with his mouth destroys his neighbor: but through knowledge shall the just be delivered.

Proverbs 11:9

Have we ever said something terribly rude or mean about another person to others? It may have been through sarcasm, trying to be funny just to get a laugh, yet not considering how our words would affect that person. Because our words cut so deeply into the individual's heart and spirit, we probably still carry the regret of having ever said them to this very day.

Our words have power. They can be used badly to hurt others deeply, or they can be used to bless and encourage. Resolve to speak life to others and to be a positive influence on everyone around us. We can do this simply by the words we say.

May we choose to be our best self each day by bringing life and encouragement to all people we encounter. Strengthen and build up and never tear down or cause any harm with our words. If we bathe the thoughts of our heart in the Scripture and meditate on the truth of God's wisdom, we will not only guard our mouth to keep us from evil, but will also pour out His words of healing and help to others, until it is not we who speak, rather Jesus speaking through us.

God's Will Always Be Good

I will sing unto the Lord because he has dealt bountifully with me.

Psalm 13:6

We will sing to the Lord because He has been so good to us. The word "bountifully" emphasizes the enormous extent of God's goodness. Our praise and adoration to Jesus should be constant. Difficult circumstances may not change, but neither does God's love for His people. Because His love is unfailing, we can rejoice, knowing that Jesus is good all the time.

The world has changed a lot over the past few years. Uncertainty and stress have affected everyone. Yet, we can look back over our lives and know assuredly that the Lord has been good to us the entire time. We can truly sing, "Through it all, I've learned to trust in Jesus...Through it all, I've learned to depend upon His Word."

God's love never fails! He has brought us through loneliness, loss, and countless other stressful and painful situations. Believers must make a choice when trouble strikes. We can despair, curse God, and succumb to fear, or we can pray and worship as we reflect on God's goodness. Regardless of what happens in the world or in our lives, we can take comfort in the fact that God is good; He has always been good; and He will always be good toward us.

Say this aloud right now, "I will sing the Lord's praise, for he has been good to me!" Take time to praise Jesus for all His goodness. We do not deserve it, but He still "deals bountifully" with us because He loves us!

Putting Out Fires

Where no wood is, there the fire goes out: so where there is no talebearer, the strife ceases.

Proverbs 26:20

Solomon used wood and fire to teach a necessary lesson on the inflammatory nature of gossip and talebearing, as opposed to the tranquility and peace that accompanies the pure words of a righteous person. As a campfire needs wood to continue burning, without a gossiper, conflict dies down. A fire can be used for good and for evil, so also the words that come out of the mouth. Our words can be wholesome and good, but words that fall from the lips of a gossip can cause great damage and harm.

Do we have friends who just seem to draw the gossip out of us? When we are around them, do we always seem to talk negatively of others? Gossip can be terribly destructive and can easily cause situations to get blown out of proportion. Decide to make the changes necessary to never become sucked into the habit of gossiping. This may require hanging around different friends who will not tempt us to gossip with them.

Take to heart the devastation and destruction that can be caused by careless speech and foolish words. Ask Jesus to reveal any adjustments we should make to stop the habit of talebearing and gossiping and to be intentional in speaking well about others. Remember this simple truth, without wood a fire will go out, and without a gossiper conflict will die down. Choose to believe the best in others and speak words of life over them. "Let the words of my mouth, and the meditation of my heart, be acceptable in thy sight, O Lord, my strength, and my redeemer" (Psalm 19:14).

Jesus Cares

Casting all your care upon him; for he cares for you.

I Peter 5:7

Scripture reminds us that the cares and concerns of this world can become a burdensome load in our lives. We cannot manage our daily problems on our own, yet the Lord's strength will be freely given, when we admit our weaknesses and inabilities, and we release all our cares and disappointments to Him. Jesus promises to bear all our burdens because of His loving-kindness and tender mercy toward us.

Life can be stressful and overwhelming at times. There are days when we deal with more than we can possibly handle on our own. When we give our cares and concerns to Jesus, He pours in peace that passes understanding, and we find godly wisdom, increased faith, supernatural love, and sufficient grace to cope with any circumstances. He cares when we feel overwhelmed. He is a God of love who cares about the most intimate details of our lives. We are never alone!

We need to surrender to Jesus the minor problems we encounter that seem so trivial, as well as the major burdens that weigh us down. Being called to cast all our worries on Jesus, does not mean giving Him selective burdens while withholding others. He cares about every part of our lives and can minister to each and every hurt, struggle, and mistake. He will strengthen us and make us fully whole. May we humble ourselves under the mighty hand of God, that He may lift us up anytime we cast ALL our cares upon Him. We are weak, but Jesus is strong!

Turn Obstacles into Opportunities

Withal praying also for us, that God would open unto us a door of utterance, to speak the mystery of Christ, for which I am also in bonds.

Colossians 4:3

Apostle Paul wrote these words while enchained in prison. He was arrested for preaching the gospel of Jesus Christ. Everything about his circumstances spoke "limitations" and "restriction." Rather than focusing on his situation, Paul remained centered on His boundless and limitless God. His prayer request was not for his own safety or to escape from prison, but that the gospel of grace and the mystery of Christ could reach more people. He continually looked for the next opportunity Jesus had for him.

Apart from the chains which may be hindering us today, understand that the God we serve has the power to set anyone free at any time. He has also empowered us and vows to never leave nor forsake us. Whenever doors of opportunity seem closed and locked, when limitations prevail, and we feel as though we walk with shackles, Jesus is still working in our lives. As Paul, keep hope alive, and continue trusting and expecting. Pray for those opportunities to present themselves. If we falter, try again and again, keep pressing forward with even greater resolve to achieve the vision and purpose that Jesus has rooted in our hearts. Paul did not know it, but his letter to the Colossians became an open door that would impact the lives of countless millions of souls for centuries.

Take responsibility to earnestly pray that God will present opportunities for doors to be opened and Christians everywhere to spread the powerful message of His kingdom and eternal hope for all. Choose to take our eyes off our surroundings and center on Jesus. Focus on the passion and vision He has deeply rooted in our heart. When things do not go as planned, remember that all challenges and adversities contain seeds of opportunity and growth. May Jesus help us to turn obstacles into opportunities and problems into possibilities.

The Final Victory is Ours!

But thanks be to God, which gives us the victory through our Lord Jesus Christ.

I Corinthians 15:57

Jesus arose triumphant in victory over sin, death, Satan, and hell, so we became triumphant in victory too! The filthy rags of our old life in Adam are replaced with the glorious garment of righteousness!

When we experience seemingly insufferable circumstances in our lives, we can become discouraged and start to feel they will never improve. The Bible tells us that we ultimately "triumph in Christ." We should never allow ourselves to become negative and bitter. Jesus has already prepared for our victory and the next phase of our lives. Faith in God does not keep us from experiencing trials and hardships, but it enables us to endure them courageously and to emerge victoriously.

True believers in Jesus Christ will claim the full and final victory over sin and death at the Rapture of the Church. Those who are still alive will be changed into His likeness, in a moment in the twinkling of an eye, and taken to be with the Lord forever. The trump of God will sound, and we will hear the shouting voice of the archangel as we, the Body of Christ, are summoned to our heavenly home!

The day is quickly approaching when this corruptible will be clothed with incorruptibility and our mortal bodies will be clothed with immortality. We will proclaim with a jubilant shout, "O death, where is thy sting? O grave, where is thy victory? We are victorious through our Lord Jesus Christ!"

Divine Protection

O Daniel, servant of the living God, is your God, whom you serve
continually, able to deliver you from the lions?

Daniel 6:20

The name Daniel has three syllables and each one in Hebrew has a meaning. "Dan" means "judge." The little "i" means "my." And "el" means "God." So, Daniel's name means "God, my judge" or "God is my judge." Each of us, like Daniel, have felt surrounded by spiteful enemies before, who wanted to throw us to the lions. It is incredibly strange how sometimes those we would take a bullet for are the ones behind the trigger ready to destroy us.

God honored Daniel's faith by protecting him from the lions and by destroying his enemies. It may seem as though the more we pray the worse things become. It may also happen to be that our friends have forsaken or even turned against us, and we feel we have been thrown into a den of lions. Be encouraged, for Jesus has the last say in the matter! God is our judge, not man. Keep centered on Jesus, trusting, and believing, for He has promised to never leave nor forsake us.

Prayer is more important than life. Daniel would rather pray than save his life. Not praying was a worse prospect to Daniel than being eaten by lions. We need a radical commitment to prayer. Can we be as committed as Daniel by declaring, "You will have to take my life before you take my prayer?" Jesus will close the lions' mouths, quash our accusers, and deliver us. Following all the hurtful accusations, the powerful Truth has come and declared, "Be free in the name of Jesus!"

Behold!

And, behold, I am with you, and will keep you in all places whither you go, and will bring you again into this land; for I will not leave you, until I have done that which I have spoken to you of.

Genesis 28:15

Frequently when God wants to emphasize an important point in Scripture, or grab our attention, He will use the word "Behold." *Behold*, I am with you! *Behold*, I will keep watch over you wherever you go! *Behold*, I will bring you back to this land! *Behold*, I will not leave you until I have done what I have promised!

Promises from God can never be broken. What a great comfort it is to realize that Jesus will be with us always and that He will indeed fulfil every promise to us. Maybe we have prayed for something, and it seems to be taking far too long to come to pass. God reminds us in this verse that He will not leave us until He has done what He has promised.

So, if we are waiting on a promise from God, know that it is coming. It may not always come in the timeframe that we desire, but His promises never fail! Jesus knows where we are and how to provide the things we need. Never quit. Never lose heart. He loves us with an everlasting love. He has a better plan for our future. Wait for Him, stay close to Him, and let Jesus lead us into the land of blessing. Let us keep our eyes on Jesus. Behold our God!

Be Made Whole Again

For I know the thoughts that I think toward you, saith the Lord, thoughts of peace, and not of evil, to give you an expected end.

Jeremiah 29:11

Jesus knows the thoughts He has toward us. He will do good and not evil. Our God is strong and mighty to save and deliver us. He is our healer, provider, and sanctifier. Jesus will uphold us with His righteous hand, for He loves us with an everlasting love.

Sometimes we may think that we have fallen so far or made such terrible mistakes that we cannot be redeemed. God is more powerful than our failures and mistakes. Rather than thinking we are damaged, broken, or are filled with distrust, we should reframe it to "I'm healing, I'm rediscovering myself, I'm starting over."

If we will humble ourselves and open our hearts in returning to Jesus, He will cleanse and renew us. The toughest battle is between hanging on and letting go. Yet, nothing in the world should prevent us from letting go of the past and beginning again. Don't give up…just start over. Jesus loves us and He specializes in giving people a fresh start!

Remember, we must not see as the world sees. Jesus holds our future in the palm of His hand. He will lead and guide us with each step, little by little by little and day by day. Leave all our burdens with Him as we keep our eyes firmly fixed upon Jesus. He has plans for our life beyond our imagination. We are God's joy and delight. He waits for us. He is standing at our heart's door knocking. Just open the door and let Him in. Jesus will enter and make us whole again.

Best Friends

A friend loveth at all times, and a brother is born for adversity.

Proverbs 17:17

The qualities of a true friend are best exemplified in the life of our Lord Jesus. He always loves, both in good and difficult times. Jesus revealed the ultimate expression of friendship when one is prepared to lay down his life for a friend or to give up his own needs and desires for the sake of a friend. Friends do not just love when it is convenient. True and lasting friendship cannot be built on dishonesty or disloyalty. Real friends speak truth in love, often when it is not what we wish to hear, yet we can grow in character and avoid making bad decisions by being receptive to their candor.

We have all been betrayed by people who we thought were our friends, those who tore our hearts open, leaving us deeply bruised and wounded internally. We wondered if we could ever trust anyone again. But Jesus taught us valuable lessons in discerning and recognizing real friends in our lives. Best friends always draw us closer to Jesus and challenge us to be our best selves. Best friends do not usually turn out to be those we would have expected.

Thank Jesus for the dear friends that He has brought into our lives and for the love and comfort we have received from them over the years. Godly counsel and encouragement are the responsibility of a good friend who loves at all times, even when it is hard. May we be good friends by showing loyalty, sensitivity, and genuine interest in them. Determine today to be there for the people around you and show them the love of Jesus. Let us challenge ourselves to push past our comfort level and really be present for our friends. We will be very pleased by how good we feel when we do.

Perfectly Loved by God

I will praise you; for I am fearfully and wonderfully made: marvelous are your works; and that my soul knows right well.

Psalm 139:14

Jesus thinks you are simply amazing! God made you for a specific calling and purpose. He has a wonderful plan for your future!

Jesus choreographs our lives, for "We know that all things work together for good to them that love God, to them who are the called according to his purpose" (Romans 8:28). Yet, far too often we do not credit Him with His work or His desire for our best. When our circumstances do not work out the way we hoped, we fail to see His greater purposes. His goal is that we grow into His image. When we reflect the life of Jesus, our faith is strong, and we love people like He loves them.

Knowing that we are wonderfully made means that we can face any situation or circumstance in faith. We know that Jesus loves us and has a wonderful plan in store. We are too valuable to Him to settle for anything less than His best for us. Realize that we can do great things for Jesus because we are important to Him and to His plan. His value of us is not based on what we do but on who we are in Him. He knows everything about us, and He still loves us! He loves us just as we are, but He desires for us to become more like Him!

The Inerrant Word of God

And that from a child you have known the holy scriptures, which are able to make you wise unto salvation through faith which is in Christ Jesus.

II Timothy 3:15

Timothy had been taught the scriptures from childhood and later mentored by the Apostle Paul. The strong foundational truths that Timothy had been taught from his mother's knee, combined with God's additional revelation through Paul, meant that this young man was firmly established on the absolute truth of God's infallible Word.

Currently however, Scripture is being distorted by liberal thinkers, pseudo-science and a worldly wisdom that has denounced God as insignificant and irrelevant. This ungodly worldview is systematically dismantling the accuracy of God's Word. The wonderful message of salvation is comparably being watered down, distorted, and discarded for another gospel. When the foundation of our Christian faith is being destroyed, what can we do? Be faithful in knowing and learning all Scriptures, which can grant us wisdom and lead us to genuine salvation, the salvation that can be found by faith in Jesus Christ alone.

Thank the Lord for those who presented wonderful gospel truth to us! Pray for the children and youth of today who are the main target of immoral and ungodly influences in this corrupt society. A society that seeks to destroy the foundational truth of the Bible. Let us work and pray to guard young hearts and minds and help lead them to the genuine Gospel Truth. "The Bible has stood the test of time because it is divinely inspired by Almighty God, written in ink that cannot be erased by any man, religion, or belief system. Through the many dark ages of man, its glorious promises have survived unchanged. That is because God's Word is pure—the beginning and the end. His written word has survived every scratch of the human pen" (Rev. Billy Graham). God's Word is forever settled in Heaven and can never be destroyed!

Have a Biblical Worldview

Set your affection on things above, not on things on the earth.

Colossians 3:2

A worldview is the framework from which we view reality and make sense of life and the world. "[It's] any ideology, philosophy, theology, movement, or religion that provides an overarching approach to understanding God, the world and man's relations to God and the world" (David Noebel).

Consider how we view the world, the way we decide, our method of making friends, and how we think and do regarding everything. Our worldview influences every part of our lives, the way we see things and our direction in life. Our worldview is like putting on a pair of glasses and peering through the lens. Of course, we can see the world as it is on the surface, although magnified depending on the strength of magnification of the lens. Yet, if we put on sunglasses, everything looks quite different, especially compared to someone not wearing them. Everything will appear darker than it actually is.

A biblical worldview is based on the infallible Word of God. When we believe the Bible is entirely true, then we allow it to be the foundation of everything we say and do. As Christians, we should see the world as Jesus does. Jesus wants to help us have the right worldview, expressing His thoughts, His ideas, and His direction for our future.

By diligently learning, applying, and trusting God's truths in every area of our lives, whether it involves watching a movie, communicating with our spouses, raising our children, or working at the office, we can begin to develop a deep comprehensive faith that will stand against the relentless tide of our culture's nonbiblical ideas. In the end, it will be our decisions and actions that reveal what we really believe. "And be not conformed to this world: but be transformed by the renewing of your mind" (Romans 12:2).

New Creation in Christ Jesus

Therefore, if any man be in Christ, he is a new creature: old things have passed away; behold, all things have become new.

II Corinthians 5:17

Despite our race, age, gender, heritage, nationality, language, education, intelligence, and ethnicity, the gospel is for each and every one of us. All who believe and receive His Spirit are "in Christ." We can become a completely new person, with a new nature and a new life in Jesus Christ. We are born of the Spirit of God, washed in His blood, and filled with His love.

Because of what Jesus did for us at Calvary, we can have perfect righteousness. Old things are passed away, and we are made a new creature born into the family of God. Our old life is replaced by a new life with a heavenly destiny and a glorious inheritance. We are seated with Jesus in heavenly places!

We are identified with Him and have become one with Him. We are united together with Him and have received the indwelling Holy Spirit to lead us and to guide us into all truth. God does not merely patch up our old life but makes us something entirely new, something unique and wonderful. We are not the old model, repaired or mended. It is not the old life reconditioned or restored. We are not simply reset, but made an entirely new person, born of the Spirit into a new creation. We identify with Christ Jesus our Lord and King!

Our regrets, mistakes, and personal failures need not follow us into the present. Past sins have caused extreme internal, interpersonal, and emotional pain and suffering for many of us. We were spiritually dying and losing hope daily. But, when Jesus reached into our hearts with His loving presence and when we said "yes" to Him, our entire being was super-transformed. The most wonderful and glorious love filled and saturated every part of our being. We have been changed! Praise God! We will never be the same again. We are a child of God!

Love the Truth

I rejoiced greatly that I found of your children walking in truth, as we have received a commandment from the Father.

II John 1:4

Walking in truth means not only to be doctrinally sound but also humble of heart, growing in grace, steadfast on the Word, delighting in the Lord, and walking in love. To live and walk in truth is to be surrendered to God, standing firm in the faith, resisting Satan, and allowing the Word of God and its truth to dwell within us richly and letting it guide our way.

"But speaking the truth in love, may grow up into him in all things, which is the head, even Christ" (Ephesians 4:15). Love is the Christian's moral temperament of heart and mind, which embraces all other virtues. It implies faith, that is founded on biblical principle, and can only be tested by correct belief. The attitude of love in general is best expressed as walking after God's commandments. Love is the practical and enlightened result of faith founded on Scripture, which naturally acts and expresses itself by following God's will in all things.

The truth about which John speaks of is the truth that was received from Jesus Christ. He is love and the love of Jesus is truly perfected in those who hold fast to the truth of His Word, submit to His will, and keep His commandments. The truth is that God was in Christ reconciling the world unto Himself. Essential to our salvation is to know the truth, protect the truth, preserve the truth, and live out the truth in our everyday life. We must apply the truth, practice the truth, preach the truth, and walk in truth each day. "Buy the truth and sell it not!" (Proverbs 23:23). Hold fast to the Truth!

Delay is Not Denial

Jesus said unto her [Mary], Said I not unto you, that, if you would believe, you should see the glory of God?

John 11:40

Jesus left immediately to come to Lazarus as soon as He had received word that Lazarus was sick; yet Lazarus died four days before Jesus could get to him. Lazarus's sister Mary said to Jesus, "Lord, if You had been here, my brother would not have died." Despite the impossible circumstances, Jesus raised Lazarus from the dead!

We live in a society where we all want things to happen now. Social media and societal influences affect our lives, even if we don't know it. We pray and pray for the desires of our heart, and when it does not happen by the time we want it to, we tend to lose hope. God makes us wait for a reason, He allows opportunities and blessings to happen in His timing. When what we want doesn't happen right away, there is a reason. Jesus will sometimes wait to fulfill a promised vision of ours until it seems utterly impossible, even dead and buried! Lazarus's sisters had hoped and prayed for their brother's healing, yet Jesus planned for a resurrection.

Jesus does not usually answer our prayers the way we intended…but keep holding on! He has something greater in mind than we could possibly have imagined. God allows us to wait so we can grow as Christians and receive greater from Him. Delay does not mean denial; it just means wait.

Be Still and Know

Be still, and know that I am God...

Psalm 46:10

Unless we take time to be still and listen, we will not hear God. Jesus cannot be heard amid noise and restlessness. The best time to listen is when there is silence. He speaks to us when we give Him our full attention and prepare ourselves to "be still" and listen.

God will never speak something that cannot be clearly confirmed in Scripture. If the Holy Spirit gives us specific direction, confirm it in His Word. Then, check it with a spiritual authority, our pastor or leader. Hear only what God speaks. The difficulty for most of us is even though we read the Bible, we do not feed from it. We become focused on learning the text, discovering the correct meaning, collecting theologies and theories, in order to speak more intelligently about God. The primary purpose for reading Scripture is not to garner information, but to draw to Jesus and to experience Him as our living God.

The Pharisaical scholars read Scripture yet did not listen to the Lord nor hear His voice (see John 5:37-39). As we read and study the Bible, move beyond information gathering to seeing, knowing, and experiencing Jesus. God's Word should motivate us to interaction with Him! We can begin by meditating on His words until His thoughts begin to shape in our minds. When we read the Bible, we read the mind of God and understand what He feels, desires, loves, and hates. Take time to be still and reflect on what Jesus is speaking, until the heart of Jesus is revealed, and our hearts are exposed.

Knowing More

I have yet many things to say unto you, but ye cannot bear them now.

Genesis 26:12

Jesus can never be fully understood through intellect. There is so much more we will never know, but some difficult questions will be answered when we are ready. Scriptural insight and knowing Jesus arise from purity of heart—love, humility, and a desire to obey His will. "Blessed are the pure in heart, for they shall see God" (Matthew 5:8). The more of His Truth we comprehend and desire to obey, the more we will know.

As we come to know and love Jesus more, we see and experience His unconditional love, mercy, compassion, and strength. We can go to Him with all our doubts, disappointments, and misunderstandings. Jesus is the only God worth knowing and having. Beside Him there is no other God!

Where is God?

And he called the name of the place Massah, and Meribah, because of the chiding of the children of Israel, and because they tempted the Lord, saying, Is the Lord among us, or not?

Exodus 17:7

When we look out over the beautiful horizons and landscapes of our world God has created, we see evidence of His presence. Yet, our hearts struggle to comprehend how One who created such splendor could allow devastating heartache. Many people today experience problems in marriage, family, work, and health, striving to see evidence of God's help. Like the children of Israel at Massah and Meribah, we may be wiping away never-ending tears and wondering if God is with us and if He truly loves us.

Jesus promises to always be near and to never forsake us. We can cope with our problems better by pausing, taking a deep breath, and choosing to acknowledge the unshakeable reality of God's presence. Now is the time to move our focus away from the obstacles in our lives toward Jesus, who will strengthen and sustain us though it all. Setting our sights on Jesus liberates us to experience His provision in unexpected ways. This enables us to not allow our carnality to form a barrier to His supernatural workings.

Jesus arrives just in time and shows up in ways beyond human comprehension. Look for Him today amidst our struggles. As the children of Israel in the desert, the rock we keep falling over may just be the tool God uses to demonstrate His sustaining presence in our lives...giving living water to our thirsty souls.

Daily and Future Provision

For as the rain cometh down, and the snow from heaven, and returns not thither, but waters the earth, and makes it bring forth and bud, that it may give seed to the sower, and bread to the eater: So shall my word be that goes forth out of my mouth: it shall not return unto me void, but it shall accomplish that which I please, and it shall prosper in the thing whereto I sent it.

Isaiah 55:10-11

The water illustration in the verse would have registered clearly with the children of Israel. Since they were dependent on seasonal rains, they had very limited water sources. The rains not only enabled crops to grow necessary food in the current year, but also provided seeds for the next year's crop. Their dependency on God for natural sustenance serves as a reminder of our need to depend on Jesus for our spiritual nourishment as well.

God already sees everything coming our way, and that means He knows exactly how to begin preparing our hearts today for tomorrow. Reading and storing Scripture deep in our hearts prepares us for the most challenging times, unexpected crises, and circumstances which shake us to the very core, leaving us to trust God to carry us through as the only option available.

God's Word not only gives us direction for today; it also sows wisdom in our heart for the future. Be intentional in spending time in His Word. Open the Bible daily to read, to receive, and to live it, whether we feel like it or not. As we apply the Word to our hearts, it becomes a part of us. May the Truth of Jesus sink deep into our hearts and sustain us through every circumstance.

Speak the Truth with Love

And thou shalt speak my words unto them, whether they will hear, or
whether they will forbear: for they are most rebellious.
Ezekiel 2:7

God was sending Ezekiel to the Israelites. He referred to them as a "most rebellious" people who may not listen. Ezekiel was encouraged not to fear the people nor what they might do, but to speak the words of God to them, regardless of whether they would listen.

We probably have some friends and family who are not following Jesus. Most know what is right, but they still choose not to live for God. Should we say something to them or not? Perhaps we see things in our world that is so wrong. Should we speak up and stand up? Should we speak truth to people, even if they will not listen and possibly ridicule us for it? What matters is that we obey the Lord by speaking what He wants us to say. We are not responsible for their will to listen, but we are responsible for the truth that Jesus tells us to speak.

In our relationships, we must not fear to speak Scriptural Truth to people. This will not always be easy to do, but we should always speak the truth with love and compassion. Our goal in speaking Truth is not to belittle or to make them feel bad. We speak it in order to lead them back to Jesus who loves them and desires His best for them.

Pray today that we will know what Jesus wants to say, that He will speak through us to others, that His love will show through us; and that they will take heed and turn to Him. Do not fear. Speak God's word in love and see Him use you to help lead others to Him.

Be Strong and Stay Alert

Watch ye, stand fast in the faith, quit you like men, be strong.

I Corinthians 16:13

Believers must stay alert, for we have numerous enemies seeking our downfall. We are surrounded with false apostles, false prophets, false teachers, deceitful workers, and doctrines of demons. These started infiltrating the early church and seem to have exploded into deceptiveness and untruth within current churches and cults who have forsaken the true gospel of Jesus Christ.

Satan seeks to invade every part of Christian life. He will even try to approach us as an angel of light, through the means of false apostles and deceitful workers, who pretend they are Christian leaders, but their faith is compromised. Scripture beckons us to be brave and strong, to never compromise our faith, and to hold fast to godliness and Truth. When courageous believers take a stand, the spines of others are often stiffened.

It can be extremely hard to stand up for Jesus when many of our "friends" and acquaintances are making choices not to align their lives with His will. How do we stand for the right when we feel as though we are the only one willing to stand? We must be strong in our relationship with Jesus. Spend time daily in His presence and Scripture. Value and protect our relationship with Him above all else. We may have to be courageous in saying and doing things differently than the majority in order to "stand fast in the faith." It is not always easy to stand for Jesus and for truth, but it is worth it! May we stay alert to the evils that surround us and never compromise the truth of the glorious gospel of Jesus, and be strong in the Lord and in the power of His might

God's Presence in the Darkness

Yea, though I walk through the valley of the shadow of death, I will fear no evil: for thou art with me; thy rod and thy staff they comfort me.

Psalm 23:4

God's presence is with us every moment, even through the darkest times. We have His blessing, favor, and protection continuously. We are seated with Jesus in heavenly places, and He is as close as the mention of His name.

Numerous people are afraid to even leave their house or take any risk for fear of what might happen. We should never let fear rule our lives. When we say to Jesus, "In You I trust," it does not mean we instantly stop sensing any fear. Trust requires choosing to act on Scriptural Truth despite the fear.

Although sometimes we feel God is a million miles away, and we cannot seem to sense His presence, we should trust and depend on His Word over our present feelings and circumstances. Speak His name, "Jesus," and we can instantly sense Him closer than the air we breathe!

The valley of the shadow of death becomes the pathway to life and peace to all who follow the Good Shepherd. Jesus will keep us from all dangers that stalk our path. May we find true comfort and protection, provision, and peace daily as we place our trust in God.

Impacting the World

For we are his workmanship, created in Christ Jesus unto good works, which God hath before ordained that we should walk in them.

Ephesians 2:20

Sometimes when we listen to or see other people's achievements that seem so meaningful and compare them to our lives, we wonder if we are making any impact at all. Amid what appears ordinary about our daily responsibilities, we can feel as though we are not accomplishing much of a greater purpose. We ponder whether this is all we should be doing with the life Jesus has given us or is there something else we should be doing.

Our ordinary can be making an extraordinary impact, if we are obedient to His Will with all we do. Our lives impact eternity without our even realizing it! Jesus is using us to bring hope to a hopeless world which so desperately needs it! A life is never wasted in the hands of the Creator! Each part has significance, and each moment has potential influence, even when we cannot see it.

Let us place our lives anew in the loving and capable hands of Jesus today and surrender ourselves to be used by Him. Ask the Lord to reveal to whom we may minister simple words of encouragement. Every single day we positively impact the world by living a genuine Christian life.

Bloom Where We Are Planted

Whoso keepeth the fig tree shall eat the fruit thereof....

Proverbs 27:18

People often become envious of others, wishing to have had a better lot in life. Jesus wants us to know that we should bloom where we are planted and cultivate the talents and life He has given us.

God will usually work on changing us before He changes our circumstances. Our current circumstances do not define us. Changing our circumstances by finding a new job, new house, or better associations cannot bring lasting joy. We may think, "if only my circumstances were different." Yet, Jesus may be saying, "If only their attitude would change."

We should allow the Lord to renew our mind, to be transformed into the mind of Christ. Resist negativity and be kind and courteous to others in spite of our current circumstances. Start praising God for all He has in store for us and bloom where we are planted. Cultivate what Jesus has given you and placed within you. Let us concentrate on putting what we have to good use rather than focusing on what we do not have. If we do this, Jesus will bless everything we put our hand to, and He will guide us onward and upward to the divine destiny He has planned for us!

Offer Jesus thanksgiving and praise from the depths of our heart today for all we have, who we are, and what He has in store for us. Be faithful over what He has entrusted to us and He will multiple it abundantly. One day, we will hear Jesus say, "Well done, good and faithful servant: you have been faithful over a few things, I will make you ruler over many things: enter into the joy of thy lord" (Matthew 25:21).

True Blessings

And all these blessings shall come on thee, and overtake thee, if thou shalt hearken unto the voice of the Lord thy God.

Deuteronomy 28:2

If we consistently honor God by obeying His Word, opportunities will present themselves to us without us even trying to make them happen. Honoring God draws the right people, resources, and influence in our lives, and the blessings of the Lord shall overtake us.

Physical as well as spiritual blessings are given by God to show where our true treasure is. Money is not the root of all evil; the love of money is. Money and wealth are simply tools for us to use. Jesus wants to know what we value. Do we want to see His kingdom manifested on Earth as it is in Heaven? He desires to free us from the addiction of allowing money to be supreme in our lives. Our security is in Jesus alone.

True blessing results from life in Jesus. God always gives His best to those who leave their choices to Him. Blessings, favor, wisdom, and validation are drawn to us like a magnet as we honor Jesus with our life. From out of nowhere opportunities will arise, our health improves, our debts are paid, and our dreams become reality. This is no coincidence. It is God's favor on our lives! His blessings have overtaken us!

Incomprehensible Love

So shall the king greatly desire thy beauty: for he is thy Lord; and worship thou him.

Psalm 45:11

The verse describes Jesus, our Lord and King, longing for us to be with Him, to worship Him. How could we possibly refrain from loving and glorifying Him who has done so much for us and who has loved us with an everlasting love?

Before we knew Jesus, many of us had chosen a path of destruction that would have destroyed any hope or dream for our future. But when we came running to Jesus, oh, what a wonderful release we felt, as we surrendered completely to Him and bathed in His amazing love!

Jesus forgave us and washed away every sin we had ever committed. We felt lighter as our hearts became pure and clean. The heavy shroud of guilt and sin fell away, replaced by a new garment of righteousness and praise. Our omniscient Savior cast all our sins into the depths of the sea! Hallelujah, we are free indeed!

The love Jesus has for us is not dependent on how we feel about ourselves, regardless of how far we may have fallen or how miserably we have failed in the past. God is love! His love does not depend on how we look or feel. His love is unselfish, beyond human understanding. The heart of Jesus is passionately set on us, and nothing can stop Him from showering us with His everlasting love!

Great Cloud of Witnesses

Wherefore seeing we also are compassed about with so great a cloud of witnesses, let us lay aside every weight, and the sin which doth so easily beset us, and let us run with patience the race that is set before us.

Hebrews 12:1

Chapter 11 of Hebrews provides the example of a great cloud of witnesses who lived by faith. Chapter 12 gives directives on how to become a witness that lives by faith, lay aside every weight and the sin which so easily entraps us, and run with patience the race that is set before us.

However, the Book of Hebrews clearly identifies the sin that does so easily beset us. Chapter 11 provides the best clue. Lack of faith in God and His Word is the sin that so easily ensnares us. Unbelief is the most besetting sin. This is the primary sin that hinders our Christian walk with the Lord the most. Believers lack faith in Scripture, because their focus is to trust in self and not to trust in Jesus.

If we will humble ourselves in faith, asking Jesus for help, He will liberate us and lift us up. If we do our part by confronting and laying aside the unbelief that is preventing us from being our best, God will do His part by helping us win the victory over it. May we daily live by faith, for we have a great cloud of witnesses as examples that we too can make it! We are victorious through Jesus Christ our Lord!

Believe God Exists

But without faith it is impossible to please him: for he who comes to God must believe that he is, and that he is a rewarder of them who diligently seek him.

Hebrews 11:6

We should come to God asking for His guidance in each situation and circumstance. However, to come to Him, we must first believe that He exists. Since we cannot see God with our eyes, we might wonder, how do I know that He really exists? The world has become contrary to God, so much of society and culture mock people of faith. Science searches for numerous reasons to doubt Jesus and all He has created. For us to have a close loving relationship with the Lord, we must believe that He exists. This can seem difficult since we cannot see Him.

God has revealed Himself through His Word, His living Word, and His written Word. Faith comes by hearing, so hear Him! We all instinctively know that God is real. We may not see Him with our eyes, but we know He is real in our heart of hearts. "For the invisible things of him from the creation of the world are clearly seen, being understood by the things that are made, even his eternal power and Godhead; so that they are without excuse" (Romans 1:20). Our world, universe, morality, and much more only make sense when we realize that Jesus Christ created everything.

When we come to Jesus, we believe that He exists. Once we believe that He exists, we can begin to enjoy the wonderful relationship He desires with each of us. Look to Jesus the Author and the Finisher of our faith, for faith comes by hearing and hearing by the Word of God. Shut out all distracting voices of the world and hear Him, listen closely from the depths of the heart and soul. Sense the nearness of His very presence now.

Rain Upon and Within Us

So shall my word be that goes forth out of my mouth: it shall not return
unto me void, but it shall accomplish that which I please, and it shall
prosper in the thing whereto I sent it.

Isaiah 55:11

In this quick-fix instantaneous generation, we always want
Jesus to intervene immediately to solve our problems and to
remove all obstacles in our path. Spending time reading the
Bible and meditating on God's Word gives more than quick
fixes. The Holy Scriptures provide instructions not just for
today, but also plants wisdom within us for the future.

Isaiah 55:10 compares God's Word to rainwater, "For as
the rain comes down, and the snow from heaven, and returns
not thither, but waters the earth, and makes it bring forth and
bud, that it may give seed to the sower, and bread to the eater."
It gives instant refreshment and nourishment for our current
situation, plus it also waters seeds to sustain us going forward.

Jesus already knows the circumstances we will face, so He
daily waters us with His Word! We should read our Bibles,
whether we feel like it or not. The more we align our lives with
God's Word, the more it will become part of us. May the truth
of each page rain on our current situation and rest deeply in
our hearts to daily sustain us.

Love Anyway

With all lowliness and meekness, with longsuffering, forbearing one another in love.

Ephesians 4:2

Apostle Paul entreats believers to live in humility and lowliness of mind. We are beseeched to be meek, mild, unselfish, gentle, patient, and kind. We are urged to patiently endure, with thanksgiving, any trying circumstances in which we may find ourselves and readily forgive one another. In doing doing so, we demonstrate the love of Jesus living inside us.

Being patient with others can be difficult. People sometimes just will not do what we want them to do! They do not say what we want them to say, nor treat us the way we want to be treated. Despite how others treat us, Scripture tells us to be patient and kind toward them. Since the love of God has been shed abroad in our hearts by the Holy Spirit, we can love everyone, despite whether they treat us well or not. We cannot control what they do, but we can control our response to them. Will we choose to respond in anger or in love?

Love is always the right decision, although it may not be easy. Practice patience with others and determine to love them daily, for we have the love of God inside us enabling us to do it.

Leave a Legacy of Faith

Who against hope believed in hope, that he might become the father of many nations, according to that which was spoken, So shall your seed be.

Romans 4:18

Abraham faced an impossible situation. When there was nothing left to hope for, Abraham still hoped. He not only believed but he also expected God to fulfill His promise. His faith resulted in Abraham becoming a father of many nations. Not only did Abraham's faith and hope bring Isaac, but a legacy also developed from his trust in the Lord.

What can we do when the situation around us feels so impossible that we feel we have no reason to hope? Despite the hopeless circumstances, we can choose to hope in Jesus and believe what He has said instead of what we see around us. Why should we hope? We have hope in Jesus despite our hopeless situation so we can help shape the next generation. Someday we will be able to tell our children that they are here because of the faith and hope we had for them. They will then pass faith on to their children. Our faith can help birth a new legacy!

The choices we make determine the type of legacy we leave. Leaving a legacy of faith involves desiring to give others our best; yet, recognizing the best we have to give is not of ourselves. We impact others to the highest degree by living a life that points them to Jesus, the Author and Finisher of our faith!

Forgive the Unforgiveable

But as for you, you thought evil against me; but God meant it unto good, to bring to pass, as it is this day, to save many people alive. Now therefore fear not: I will nourish you, and your little ones. And he comforted them, and spoke kindly unto them.

Genesis 50:20-21

In Genesis 50, Joseph forgives his brothers for cruelly and unmercifully selling him as a slave into Egypt. His brothers' degree of jealousy toward him was so great that they nearly killed him but decided to sell Him instead. Joseph was left separated from the brothers for many years. They finally meet again where Joseph forgives his brothers and iterates how God used their evil plan to rescue not only His family, but also the entire Israelite nation. Surprisingly all is forgiven.

We can change people's opinion of us with kindness. God does not want us to live our lives vengeful in getting back at those who hurt us. Living with bitterness and anger only hinders us from a successful and joyful life. Let us demonstrate kindness to others that do not deserve it. May we be forgiving and merciful to anyone who has wronged us.

Being a Christian means to forgive the unforgivable because Jesus has forgiven the unforgivable in us. Forgiveness is the saving of the heart. Forgiveness spares the cost of anger, the expense of hatred, the price of souls.

Kings and Priests of God

And has made us unto our God kings and priests: and we shall reign on the earth.

Revelation 5:10

Jesus has made us kings and priests unto Him! As kings we have a responsibility to provide leadership for others. His redeemed are also priests. As such, we have a duty to direct people to God, to teach the Word of God, to counsel, and to pray for others. The Lord desires for us to carry ourselves with confident expectation, knowing that we are royalty in Him. This does not mean for us to be conceited, but humbled and grateful that God has appointed us.

Jesus did not create an exclusive order of priests, such as the Levites. Instead, He made all believers priests unto God. "But you are a chosen race, a royal priesthood, a holy nation, a people for his own possession, that you may proclaim the excellencies of him who called you out of darkness into his marvelous light" (I Peter 2:9).

When we begin seeing ourselves as kings and priests in Him, we will never feel intimidated or inferior again. The King of kings and Lord of lords has crowned us with righteousness, glory, rejoicing and life (II Timothy 4:8; I Peter 5:4; I Thessalonians 2:19; Revelation 2:10). Royalty is our identity. Servanthood is our mission. Intimacy with God is our source of empowerment and life. Royalty resides not in vain spectacle nor pride, but in great virtues and character.

Hope and Joy in Jesus

The hope of the righteous shall be gladness: but the expectation of the wicked shall perish.

Proverbs 10:28

The hope of the righteous brings joy! Righteous believers experience trials, but we do not have any reason to despair. Hope in this verse refers to "confident expectation." We know our trials will end someday. We anticipate that day, and our hope enables us to be joyful despite challenging circumstances. The unrighteous, who rely on themselves and the false philosophies of the world rather than Jesus, are doomed for disappointment and condemnation. But we rejoice because we have an endless hope!

Being a Christian does not mean everything is great. Things may not be going our way. We may be dealing with family issues, our friends may currently be unfriendly, or coworkers may be sabotaging our work or reputation. Yet, we can still have joy unspeakable and full of glory on the inside! True joy is formed in the midst of the difficult seasons of life. Joy is not the absence of suffering; it is the presence of Jesus. "You will show me the path of life: in your presence is fulness of joy..." (Psalm 16:11).

Our joy is not based on whether everything is going perfectly in our lives. Rather, our joy comes from an intimate relationship with Jesus. Knowing Jesus and abiding with Him is where we find joy.

We have been made righteous by God. Even our worst days cannot steal our joy, for in Him we find worth, meaning, and everlasting peace and joy! It is His joy that remains in us that makes our joy full. Jesus is our true source of joy!

Abiding Peace Within

These things I have spoken unto you, that in me you might have peace. In the world you shall have tribulation: but be of good cheer; I have overcome the world.

John 16:33

Jesus never ignores the desperate cries of His children who cry out to Him daily. He understands the fears we face and the doubts that flood our minds, even when all that is seemingly safe, secure, and stable gets thrown into frenzied chaos. He promises peace to those who trust in His Word and who abide in His love. Let not your heart be troubled!

When life is stressful, we can choose to be at peace. Being at peace does not mean that our circumstances are perfectly aligned. The peace that Jesus gives abides within our hearts, independent of all that is going on around us. We may be dealing with extremely difficult circumstances, yet we can choose His peace amid them.

Peace comes when there is no cloud between us and God. The only way we experience peace which passes understanding is to abide in Jesus, in fellowship with Him, in sweet communion with Him, resting in the promises He has taught us in His Word. We can be at peace even if our circumstances are not perfect. No matter what may happen, we are safe in the everlasting arms of Jesus!

Acknowledge Jesus in Everything

In all your ways acknowledge him, and he shall direct your paths.

Proverbs 3:6

It is not in one way, some ways, many ways, nor most ways that we are to acknowledge God. We are compelled to acknowledge Him in all our ways. When our heart and soul is set on Jesus in all our ways, we discover that He truly is guiding our path in the best possible direction.

Often, we make following Jesus and His plan for our lives too complicated. We contemplate so heavily on trying to determine precisely what He wants us to do that we do not move forward in making decisions merely because we are waiting to hear from God. Jesus does speak to us in astonishing ways at times, but most often, following Him should seem ordinary.

This verse provides insight into following the Lord. We are simply to think about Him in all our ways and continually consider what pleases Him rather than our self-gratification. Following Jesus and hearing from Him need not be spectacular. It can often be simply ordinary. It requires us to be quiet and still for a few minutes in thinking about Him and what He wants. He will direct our paths if we are willing to listen. When our love for Him becomes the single central longing of our heart, then we will find that He is there leading, directing and communing with us in love.

Soar with Faithfulness

And all things, whatsoever you shall ask in prayer, believing, you shall receive.

Matthew 21:22

Jesus is the God of abundance, who gives us much more than we deserve. David said, "My cup runneth over…" God wants us to have an overflowing life, in which everything we touch will prosper as we align our life with His Word and His will. More than our success Jesus wants faithfulness.

After God sees that we are faithful and disciplined on the spiritual, financial, and relationship levels, He will usually advance us to the next level. "Delight thyself also in the Lord: and he shall give thee the desires of thine heart" (Psalm 37:4). Prosperity does not bring joy, faithful relationship with Jesus Christ brings genuine joy.

Only those who are rooted in Jesus Christ are able to prosper and still have joy in every situation. If we want to prosper, first we must prosper in Him. Hold faithfulness and sincerity as first principles, then soar with wisdom and surmount with dignity.

Love Ourselves and Others

...You shall love your neighbor as yourself.

Matthew 22:39

David Jesus accentuated and exhibited love. It is His fundamental nature (I John 4:16). The Spirit of God pours it into our hearts (Romans 5:5) and produces it as the fruit of God's presence in us (Galatians 5:22-23). Jesus emphasized it would be our identifying characteristic as His disciples (John 13:35). This is why we are to not only love God and others; we must love ourselves too!

Having low self-esteem is like walking through life with a ball and chain around our leg. We carry ourselves the way we view ourselves. If we cannot love ourselves or are discontent with who we are on the inside, this will bleed over causing problems in relationships with others or will keep us from forming new and healthy relationships.

In order to love others, we first need to love ourselves. People pick up on how we view ourselves. So, we should stop focusing on our imperfections and begin loving ourselves in a healthy way, being grateful for how our Lord has made us. This will create new opportunities, give us new friends, and increased favor with God. "I will praise you; for I am fearfully and wonderfully made..." (Psalm 139:14).

Need Wisdom, Just Ask!

If any of you lack wisdom, let him ask of God, who gives to all men liberally, and upbraideth not; and it shall be given him.

James 1:5

In Chapter one of James, we learn it is pretty easy to live as a Christian when all is well. However, it can become quite difficult when life's trials come at us in full force. During such times, we can get thrown off course, become discouraged, and begin to doubt. With God's wisdom, we can navigate through these trials so that we not only endure, but joyfully endure (James 1:2). By wisdom, James refers to the empowerment and skill that enables us to live obediently before the Lord in the midst of trials. The result will be a truly beautiful life that glorifies Jesus.

Life is full of pitfalls and snares, and we often make bad decisions. But it is comforting to know that no matter what trials we may be called upon to face, or what foolish choices we have made in the past, we can go to Jesus and ask Him for godly insight and spiritual understanding, and He promises to give us all that is needed. If we are facing trials, especially temptations, what should we do? Ask Jesus for help and wisdom!

Let us never complain or blame God but entreat His guidance and help. If we have not asked Him for wisdom, ask Him to show us ways we can make our life less stressful, further productive, and more fulfilled. Our main priority is intimacy with Jesus. His wisdom will flow through our every thought if we will seek Him with our whole heart! May Jesus grant us the wisdom we need to face the future with joy.

Be A Peacemaker

Blessed are the peacemakers: for they shall be called the children of God.

Matthew 5:9

The Prince of Peace not only calls believers to be recipients of peace but blesses those who are bestowers of peace. We demonstrate spiritual maturity whenever we ignore or forgive an insult and not lose our cool. Jesus said, "Blessed are the peacemakers," not those who are correct.

Too often breaches are widened, bitterness is increased, and anger is provoked. One little spark of suspicion or dislike can stimulate an evil progression. One careless word can result in a rift that drifts into irreconcilability. An impulsive action can cause the ripping apart of a blessed union. O' how sad!

"If it be possible, as much as lies in you, live peaceably with all men" (Romans 12:18). Sometimes to keep the peace, we may need to allow the other person to think he/she is right. We could battle with a friend to win or prove we are right and risk destroying the friendship. Think about it; God could be asking us to lay aside our ego and be a peacemaker today.

We should sincerely desire to become peacemaking children of the Lord with all diligence. Our world desperately needs more peacemakers, healers, restorers, and lovers of people. May Jesus give us wisdom to know when we should be silent and simply ignore something that has irritated us to be a peacemaker. Now is the time we should be peacemakers in a world of beauty marred by strife. Now is the accepted time, for tomorrow could be too late!

God Is

In the beginning God created the heaven and the earth.

Genesis 1:1

The first verse in the Bible declares "In the beginning, God..." Anything that does not begin with God will not stand. Science has tried to disprove Him for centuries. God never stoops to human intellect to prove Himself. God IS. He reveals Himself in His Word, through His names, His character, and His Truth. We are simply to believe what God says about Himself in order to experience His Spirit in our lives.

Jesus never seeks to prove He exists. He simply states, I AM. I AM the Way, the Truth, and the Life. I AM the Resurrection and the Life. Before Abraham was, I AM. I AM the Beginning and the Ending, the First and the Last. I AM that I AM! Apart from Me there is no other God! No scientific experiment can prove His existence, yet the Heavens declare the glory of God and the firmament shows His handiwork!

A central concept we must settle in our walk with Jesus is that He is the Creator. "All things were made by him; and without him was not anything made that was made" (John 1:3). There is no higher power than Jesus. Seeing Him as our Creator is foundational to our faith. Rather than destroy us for our sins and failures, the Omnipotent and Omniscient Creator of the universe decided to love us and to extend His mercy so we could know Him in the power of His resurrection! Praise His Holy Name!

Not God's Fault

*And unto Adam he said, Because thou hast hearkened unto the voice of
thy wife, and hast eaten of the tree, of which I commanded thee, saying,
Thou shalt not eat of it: cursed is the ground for thy sake; in sorrow shalt
thou eat of it all the days of thy life; Thorns also and thistles shall it bring
forth to thee; and thou shalt eat the herb of the field; In the sweat of thy
face shalt thou eat bread, till thou return unto the ground; for out of it
wast thou taken: for dust thou art, and unto dust shalt thou return.*

Genesis 3:17-19

Adam sinned willfully, having abandoned his leadership
position. Sin is disobedience to God and failure to do
what God has commanded. Because of his sin, the proceeding
generations have been cursed with burdensome labor just to
stay ahead, yet paradoxically for our ultimate benefit. We are
perfected in trials, suffering, hardship, and hard work, all of
which we should consider a blessing from God to rescue us
from sin.

People often look around at the war, chaos, and other
terrible things happening in our world and ask, "How could a
loving God allow such dreadful things to happen?" Based on
this erroneous conception, they decide not to put their faith in
Jesus. Consider this. God is not responsible for the bad things
that happen, but they are a result of sin. Because of Adam's sin,
the world is cursed, and it is not the good place that God
created originally. This is the reason we see sickness, death,
suffering, and many of the bad things in the world. Our world
is fallen and broken. Satan, our real adversary, is constantly
going about as a roaring lion desiring to kill, steal, and destroy,
and seeking whomever he might devour (see John 10:10; I
Peter 5:8).

Realize today that the bad things happening in the world is not God's fault. Our world simply is not the same good place our loving Jesus created originally. Yet, if we live for Him, He promises someday to bring us to a wonderful place beyond this world, "Let not your heart be troubled: ye believe in God, believe also in me. In my Father's house are many mansions...I go to prepare a place for you" (John 14:1-2).

Deeply Rooted in Jesus

And he shall be like a tree planted by the rivers of water...

Psalm 1:3

Individuals who are identified as truly blessed are those who delight in Scripture and meditate day and night on God's Word. Their roots are deeply embedded in the truth of God's Word, and their sustenance flows from multiple streams of God's eternal provision.

If a tall and strong tree's root system does not grow more than one foot underground, powerful winds can come and blow it over. This rule is true for our lives as well. When storms of life rage against us—problems, chaos, or temptation—we must be deeply rooted in God and His Word in order to keep standing strong and to survive the storm. We become easily offended, discouraged, and distressed when we are not deeply rooted. We may become quickly moved by our emotions and irritated by something someone said or did or by feeling we have been treated unfairly. However, when we are deeply rooted in Jesus, realizing He is in control, the storms of life can rage while we keep standing strong and tall in the name of Jesus!

We will not wither when seasons of difficulty and drought come to test our faith. We will not be overwhelmed by the enemy's wiles, for we are covered by the armor of God. We will not be unsettled by problems and pain, for we are anchored to the Rock of our salvation and protected under the shadow of His wings. Beautiful, strong, and fruitful characterizes a life rooted and grounded in the life and love of Jesus. May we remain rooted and nourished in good ground.

A Good World

And God saw every thing that he had made, and, behold, it was very good...

Genesis 1:31

When God created the world, everything He created was good. Everything from the sky to animals and from the oceans to mountain peaks are all part of His wonderful creation. The Earth is so complex and magnificent. The way He placed everything in balance so that human, animal, and plant life could sustain is simply amazing. God's creation is miraculous! Take time to look around outside and see some of what He has created.

We can easily see the imbalance created by humans in our world today—hate, war, hunger, disease, and pain—and wonder how did it become so bad? Sin has brought far too much misery and a curse upon the world. All the bad we see around us is not what God saw as good, but it all has resulted from sin and disobedience to Him. Today's world is not the same as when He created it. The one He created was very good!

Although the world has been cursed by sin, the wonderful news is that Jesus promises a new Heaven and a new Earth one of these days! We have eternal hope in Jesus! May we move our focus from the darkness man has created in the world and turn our eyes to Jesus, the true Light of the World, who will one day carry us to our perfect and eternal home in glory!

Power of Our Words

And the tongue is a fire, a world of iniquity: so is the tongue among our members, that it defiles the whole body, and sets on fire the course of nature; and it is set on fire of hell.

James 3:6

James makes it evident that the words we say reveal our true nature. An unbridled tongue can do tremendous damage to ourselves and to others. It is likened to an unchecked fire that can burn down an entire forest of trees. As fallen individuals, our nature is sinful and destructive. Therefore, we need Jesus to change us.

Jesus hears every word we speak when we bless, compliment, and encourage others. He also knows when we complain, criticize, and gossip. The Bible says that we will reap what we sow. If we sow negativity, disrespect, disharmony, and condemnation, we will reap the same. However, if we sow mercy, compassion, love, and kindness, this is also what we will reap. Our tongue is a fire that can be dangerous or delightful. A single word can start severe conflict or promote harmony.

We can change the course of our lives and the lives of others with our words. Let us ignite good fires of hope, love, passion, and unity today with our words. May the words of our mouth, the meditation of our hearts, the attitude of our soul, and the motive behind all we say and do, be honoring to Christ Jesus our Lord!

Jesus Gave His All

For all have sinned, and come short of the glory of God.

Romans 3:23

After Adam's fall and disobedience in the Garden of Eden, God knew people would continually fall into sin and mess up their lives. Despite how hard we try to be righteous on our own, we cannot earn God's love or salvation. Everyone has sinned and come short of His glory. This is why He planned from the beginning of the world a path to salvation for us. Jesus is ready and waiting to forgive us if only we will come to Him asking for mercy and forgiveness for our sins.

Jesus loved us enough to give His life for us. He had such compassion to restore us back to Him that He was willing to pay the ultimate price. "Greater love hath no man than this, that a man lay down his life for his friends" (John 15:13).

Jesus values us more than we value ourselves. He loved us so much that He gave His life on Calvary to free us from sin. No longer shall sin have dominion over us! By faith we have moved from the kingdom of darkness into the kingdom of light, from the kingdom of death to the kingdom of life, from the kingdom of sorrow to the kingdom of joy, from the kingdom of fear to the kingdom of love. Hallelujah!

Our Greatest Defense

No weapon that is formed against thee shall prosper; and every tongue that shall rise against thee in judgment thou shalt condemn. This is the heritage of the servants of the Lord, and their righteousness is of me, saith the Lord.

Isaiah 54:17

A life rooted in the gospel of Jesus Christ is immovable and unshakable. When we build our life on God's Word a strong foundation is formed which provides stability and power for enduring deliverance and development (see Romans 1:16).

Even if we are walking through an extremely difficult season currently, we can be encouraged in Jesus and hold to His promises. We can invite Him into our area of need, whether it be healing, provision, or relationship, and we can trust Him to work everything for our good. We can run to Jesus and cast all our cares on Him, because He truly loves and cares deeply for us.

The last line of the verse emphasizes our righteousness is from the Lord Jesus Himself. The clearer we comprehend our righteousness in Him, the greater we will experience His promise of being an overcomer of any attacks by the enemy. If we are not rooted in His righteousness, Satan's weapons will be successful against us--guilt, condemnation, fear, depression, and numerous other weapons.

We must heed to the True Gospel of Jesus Christ, not the worldly pseudo-Christianity of our day which encourages unrighteousness. The Lord promises that no weapon formed against us shall prosper! Every false accusation and malicious lie and allegation we shall condemn! Let us depend on the True Gospel for His protection from all dangers, knowing that the angel of His presence encamps around all who are His. Let us rest on the assurances of His presence through all of life's difficulties.

War Against the Soul

Dearly beloved, I beseech you as strangers and pilgrims, abstain from fleshly lusts, which war against the soul.

1 Peter 2:11

Poor choices can wreak havoc on our lives. Our desperate struggle and uncontrollable carnal cravings wage war against the soul. Satan tries to whisper in our minds that we will never be free from this battle, that we will always be susceptible to this sinful desire, and we will never find deliverance. Yet, victory is possible in Jesus!

When the enemy presents things before us, realize He is using it to lure us away from God. It may be alcohol, drugs, inappropriate relationships, overspending, excessive food cravings, or any other thing which he can use to entice us into a position where we lose self-control. He is not particular about the method, only the result in bringing us down.

Being controlled by anything other than God is wrong. Jesus desires to lead us in the paths of righteousness for His name's sake. Even if we have been battling something for years, dig past the surface to the root of the problem. We will find a loving compassionate God, one who knows the weaknesses that are keeping us from pursuing Him wholeheartedly. Surrender all to Jesus and allow Him to lead and guide us into all truth and righteousness. Daily discipline to His Word, prayer, and leading will produce freedom in our lives. When carnal struggles wage a war against our soul, may Jesus give us the strength we need to overcome and to love Him more than anything or anyone.

Jesus Searches the Hidden Parts

*Behold, you desire truth in the inward parts: and in the hidden part you
shall make me to know wisdom.*

Psalm 51:6

Jesus Throughout the course of our spiritual journey Jesus
deals with deep-rooted parts of us. He reaches until He
touches the very depths of the soul, the hidden secret
chambers that we have revealed to no one. He goes right into
our innermost being. Jesus is continually working toward the
most inward part.

Before we can conquer hidden sin, hurt, or failure, we
must face up to it. Hidden things poison and spread like a
cancer in our lives. Jesus expects honesty and truth internally,
"in the hidden part." Hidden sin does not simply disappear on
its own. He will meet us with His merciful provision and
restoring touch when we sin and do wrong. He will meet us in
His loving favor. However, Jesus will not stop until He pursues
the problem to the innermost secret place of our being. There
He will register His work of grace and redemption, so we may
truly be free and so the sin or iniquity will no longer have
dominion over us.

May truth be in our "hidden part" daily. Ask Jesus to
create in us a clean heart, a renewed spirit, and to restore His
joy of salvation unto us (see Psalm 51:10, 12). He has set His
heart and love upon having us, who are partakers of the divine
nature, having escaped the corruption that is in the world.
"Because he hath set his love upon me, therefore will I deliver
him: I will set him on high, because he hath known my name"
(Psalm 91:14).

The End

Made in the USA
Columbia, SC
20 September 2022

67292755R00117